WOODWORKING
THE COMPLETE GUIDE

40 PROJECTS

JOHANNES POULARD

The Complete Guide to Woodworking

40 Woodworking Projects for Your Home

Furniture, Cabinets, Tables, Chairs, and Dressers and Chests with Drawers

Johannes Poulard

Preface: What you can do with wood. What is the intent of this book? Basically, you will learn about the importance of woodworking and how you can improve your home and save tons of money by simply making many of the things you end up spending hundreds of dollars buying. You will also learn how you can add your personal touch when learning woodworking.

Chapter One: Starting with the basics: what tools you need, what woodworking is and how it differs from woodcarving, knowing how to properly nail or screw wood together without splitting the wood. You will also learn what types of screws and nails are needed for different aspects of woodworking.

Chapter Two: Simple cabinet making: learning how to make cabinets for your kitchen, how to properly hang them, using puck lighting for overhead cabinet soffits and inside the cabinet. You will also learn how to make wood cabinet doors with fancy glass inside.

Chapter Three: Shelving: learn how to make all kinds of different shelves to store all kinds of different things, from heavy duty basic wood shelving for your basement, garage, or tool shed. Learn about concrete nails and how you need to use them if you plan to nail wood to a concrete wall or floor, especially needed for shelving in your basement. You will also learn how to make nice looking book shelves and lighted shelves for your trinkets and collectibles for your den, living room, parlor, or dining room.

Chapter Four: Wardrobe Closets and Armoires: Learn how to build a fancy wardrobe closet cabinet or armoire for your bedroom and guest rooms in your home. This project is ideal for people who live in small houses with little closet space. In this chapter you will also learn how to build a hutch with glass doors and puck lights to help display your fine china, elegant silverware, and more.

Chapter Five: Dressers, desks, and other furniture with drawers: you will learn this complicated part of woodworking. Mastery in woodworking means you need to make drawers and have them be compatible with the furniture you make them for. You will learn about dove tailing and other ways to fasted the pieces of wood together and make a drawer which will not come apart.

You will also learn how you can attach a special track which your drawers can slide open and closed on.

Chapter Six: Tables and chairs: The epitome of furniture. You will learn how to build any kind of table and chair from the simple to the elegant. Learn how to build your own dining room table and chairs, bar stools, rocking chairs, porch swings, kiddy tables and chairs.

Chapter Seven: Hanging doors and windows: Learn how to hang your own doors and windows. You will learn alternatives to double-hung windows. Make Russian and European style windows with the winter fortochka. Learn how to make your own doors, whether single doors, double doors, or doors with transom windows. Learn what woods make the best window frames for outdoor windows.

Chapter Eight: Boat building: Learn how to make an actual wooden boat, such as skiffs, scows, and row boats. Learn how to make a basic sailboat with a removable dagger board for use at the beach on a lake or river. Learn about special marine glues and other waterproofing techniques. Fun project to do with the kids.

Chapter One

Starting with the Basics

When undertaking any woodworking project, you will need to know basics of woodworking. This also includes safety tips for use of power tools and knowing what the names of different tools are and what they are used for. In this chapter, you will learn the following:

A. **Basic woodworking tools** needed for any basic project. These are the simplest of tools for the bare minimum of woodworking. These include both power and manual saws, drills, hammers, and power nailers.
B. **Woodworking and woodcarving** and how they differ. You will learn that woodcarving is a type of woodworking, but it is more of an art form and less of a functional aspect of woodworking. For those of you who are interested in incorporating woodcarving in your woodworking, you will learn the basic tools you will need for two dimensional woodcarving and you will also learn about basic chip carving. We will briefly cover relief and three dimensional woodcarving and what it is.
C. **Nails and screws** and how to distinguish them by size, what each type of nail and screw is designed to do, etc. You will understand the penny system and how it gauges the size of nails and what each penny nail is used for. You will also learn about shingling nails, finish nails, drywall nails, and more.
D. **Proper nailing and screwing pieces of wood together** without splitting the wood. Many people get frustrated with wood splitting when nailing and screwing them together. Learn how to drill the proper sized hole for most vital wooden structures. You will also learn how to use finish nails for trim, baseboards, and other detail work so they won't be visible.

Basic Woodworking Tools
When doing any woodworking project, you need to use the right tools. Here you will learn the proper tools, both power and manual tools. You will learn about power and hand saws, power drills, chisels, hammers, and power nailers.

Power saws are the backbone of any woodworking project. Basically, there are many different power saws which are used on a regular basis for different aspects of woodworking. The basic power saws you will be using are mentioned in depth below.

The skill saw is your basic power saw which you can use for almost every project. The skill saw is used to cut planks, boards, plywood, and more. Skill saws are also designed to have a mitered plate which you can adjust to cut at different angles for those difficult areas. See Figure One below to see a typical skill saw.

Figure One: The skill saw

Basically, the skill saw is operated by holding the top of it with your hand. The blade of the skill saw is circular and is replaceable. When the blade goes dull, you need to replace it. It can be difficult to sharpen and not very many sharpeners can sharpen blades. You can easily get blades for your skill saw at any Menard's, Lowe's, Home Depot, or any other large home improvement.

Basic uses for the skill saw are primarily for cutting 2X4s, 2X6s, 2X10s, and 2X12s. Skill saws are also used to cut small boards, pieces of plywood, and other on site cutting of wood.

The power miter saw is a circular saw which is attached to an arm which hangs over a ruled cutting board with a fence to hold the wood being cut in place. The job of a miter saw is to be able to cut wood at different angles. You can rotate the blade arm to a given angle. By the rotation lever, you have a protractor which shows an angle marker which shows you the degree of the angle you are cutting the wood.

Uses of the power miter saw are primarily for cutting wood in angles to make complex corners, 45 degree angles for right angle corners, and more.

The table saw is a special circular saw which is set on a table like structure. Most of the table saws are placed on a table which is about three feet by three to six feet. Some table saws also have the ability of setting up a ripping fence and you can also attach a safety pusher which looks similar to a T-square. The safety pusher keeps the wood you are cutting straight.

Uses for the table saw include ripping boards, cutting large pieces of plywood in a straight edge. Ripping boards is basically cutting a board or plank in half to fit it into a tight spot. Basically, an example of ripping is cutting a 2X4 in half, making two 2X2s.

Sawzall is a special power saw which is designed to cut through old wood which needs to be removed. This looks like an oversized jigsaw and the typical sawzall blade can range from six to eight inches. The primary use of a sawzall is to cut through headers and footers which need to be removed for additions and other major remodeling projects.

Hand Saws
Hand saws might be needed from time to time. Typically, the type of hand saw you will need is your basic wood saw and can be used in areas where power tools cannot.

Drills
Drills are almost as important as saws. Though manual drills are available, most people now use power drills and many power drills can come with a wide variety of drill bits and screw driver bits. Some of the famous brands of power drills which we recommend and can be found at any home improvement store which sells power tools include Makita, DeWalt, Ryobi, and Bosch. Makita, DeWalt, and Bosch are the best.

Some power drills need to constantly be plugged into a wall outlet, but others do have a set of rechargeable batteries. Depending on where you are doing your woodworking at, you might want to get a drill with a rechargeable battery pack. When purchasing a battery drill, you might want to get two or three battery packs for the drill, though a drill battery can hold its charge for a long time. Lithium ion batteries are the best because they can operate a large amperage tool, like a power drill and maintain a charge for several hours.

Different drill bits include the typical bits which look like small augers. These are the typical drill bits you will use most of the time. These are primarily used for drilling pilot holes for nails and screws (see below). These drill bits can also be used for other functions, such as running support wire, trellis wire, and more.

Saw drill bits are the round drill bits which are a large circular shape and have teeth, like a saw blade. These bits are used to drill large holes into the wood and can be used to run thick 220 V wiring for refrigerator, stove, dishwasher, or washer and dryer outlets. These saw drill bits can also be used for a variety of other projects also.

Spade bits are drill bits which are shaped like a spade and have a point. These are also designed drill large holes and many contractors will use spade bits to drill holes for wiring, plumbing, and other lines for home construction.

Flat head screw driver bits are designed to quickly drive flat head wood screws which have a single line in its head.

Phillips screw driver bits are designed to drive Phillips screws into wood. Phillips screws are the most difficult screws to drive in because of the cross head. Many Phillips screw driver bits are magnetic because Phillips screws need to have the bit in just right otherwise they strip. **Hex-head bits** are used to screw hex-head screws and bolts. These kinds of screws are used to screw wood to concrete.

Hammers
One of the most important tool you can have for most woodworking projects are hammers. There are different varieties of hammers which can be used for different projects.

There are different types of hammers but the most common is the carpenter's hammer. This is what you think of as a hammer. This hammer has a round end at one side of the head for driving nails in and a claw on the other side of the head incase you have to pull a bent nail out. See Figure Two below to understand what the conventional carpenter's hammer looks like. You can also get a smaller hammer which looks like a carpenter's hammer for finish nails.

Figure Two: The two types of carpenter's hammers

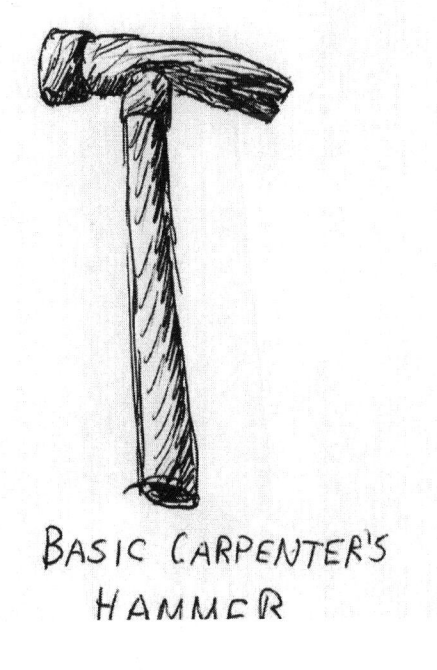

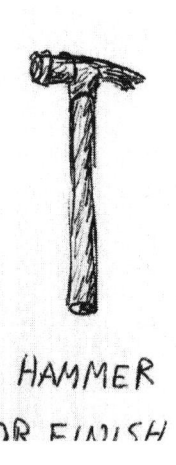

BASIC CARPENTER'S HAMMER   HAMMER FOR FINISH

The ball ping hammer is a hammer which has the typical round flat end of the head for driving nails in and a ball ping on the other side of the head. See Figure Three. Uses for the ball ping hammer are typically light nailing, such as finish nails.

Figure Three: The ball ping hammer

Hand held sledge hammer is a sledge hammer head on a small handle which you can drive with one hand. This is a heavier hammer and is usually used for nailing landscape timbers or old railroad ties together with large spike nails for wooden retaining walls or planters.

Figure Four: Hand held sledge hammer

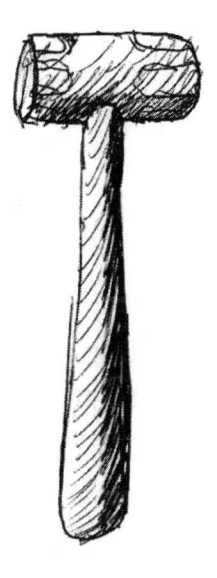

The heavy sledge hammer is a powerful tool and has a longer handle which is designed to be swung with the force of both hands and arms. This is primarily a demolition hammer. Used mostly in remodeling projects where walls need to be broken out. This sledge hammer has enough torque to be able to hammer apart old 2X4s and even 2X12s. Great tool to use in combination with a cat's paw. See Figure Five below about a cat's paw.

The cat's paw is a type of pry bar which also has a claw on it, much like the one on a carpenter's hammer. The cat's paw also has a flat head at the other end of the bar. The cat's paw is very handy in demolition work as you can use it to pry apart boards which are nailed or screwed together. The flat end of the cat's paw works much like that of an ordinary pry bar and you can use that to pry apart some of the more stubborn parts of the structure you want to demolish.

Figure Five: The cat's paw

The power nailer is basically replacing the hammer in many respects. There are different kinds of power nailers on the market and you can find them at any Menard's, Lowe's, Home Depot, or any other major home improvement store. Most power nailers function with an air compressor and use forced air to drive the nails into the wood. Other power nailers are actually considered firearms, as they have small bullets with actual gun powder with the nails at the top of the shell. These are sometimes used by professional contractors.

Woodworking and Woodcarving
Woodworking is basically working with wood in general. This can also include woodcarving, however, woodworking can be both artistic and functional, whereas woodcarving is primarily artistic and is primarily used to decorate wood features in a home or on furniture.

Basically, if you want to learn more in depth about woodcarving, you will have to get resources to teach you the basics to the more complicated. We write this book primarily for woodworking projects with carpentry in mind, but we do encourage you to adventure out of the norm and learn the basics. One thing is for sure, if you learn and are able to carve your own designs, you will have some unique projects when you incorporate that with what you learn in this book.

Two dimensional woodcarving is woodcarving which is two dimensional. This includes chip carving, which is the simplest form of two dimensional woodcarving and it is primarily a series of geometric shapes carved together to create a design. Chip carving is very common in folk art of many different cultures.

Relief carving is another type of two dimensional woodcarving. This is designed to make two dimensional woodcarving have depth and look three dimensional.

Three dimensional woodcarving is special woodcarving which is used in making three dimensional objects out of wood, such as statues, figurines, bowls, musical instruments, and more. Three dimensional woodcarving is by far more complicated than two dimensional woodcarving as it requires more carving and shaping of the wood block you are working with. You can incorporate three dimensional woodcarving to make interesting pieces for the tops of your bedposts, or other ornamentation on your woodwork.

The lave is an ideal tool to carve ridges and round out bedposts for a bunk or princess bed, which will be covered later in this book. That chapters on beds and furniture will cover the use of the lave and how you can make beautiful things.

Nails and Screws
Knowing nails and screws is important for any major woodworking project. Along with nails and screws, you will also have to know about wood glues which are sometimes necessary together with nails and screws for a strong bond. Glues will be covered below about nailing and screwing wood pieces together.

Nail size is often referred to penny, especially for galvanized nails used in home construction and remodeling. Other smaller nails are used for roofing, finishing, and nailing light features to your woodworking projects. In some cases, you may want to have screws for a stronger bond. Screws will be covered below.

12 penny nails are the largest galvanized nails you can get and they are primarily for home construction. You will want to use 12 penny nails for stud-plate construction, as these nails will penetrate in the wood deep enough to have a strong hold between the plate and the stud (You will learn this later in the chapter covering home construction and remodeling).

Some 12 penny nails are twisted also. These are good nails for home construction as they twist as you drive them in and give a stronger hold and are less likely to pull out than the straight 12 penny nails.

Eight penny nails are primarily used to nail plywood or particle board to the floor joists and to the studs for walls. These nails are not as long as the above mentioned 12 penny nails and should not be used for foam board. Those need a special nail with a special green plastic lip to hold the foam board in place.

Roofing nails tend to look more like oversized galvanized thumbtacks than nails. They are short with a wide head. These nails are used to nail tar paper and asphalt shingles to the plywood roof of a home. You will learn how to do this in the chapter about home construction and remodeling.

Drywall nails are designed to nail drywall or sheet rock to the studs when finishing a room. What exactly is drywall? Well, basically, drywall is gypsum board. It is gypsum, the same material used to make plaster and is a rather weak material, thus when hanging a picture on a wall, you want to make sure a nail is in the stud.

Basically, drywall nails are made from a lighter metal than the traditional galvanized nails and when you hammer them in, you want to make a dimple around the nail. This allows you to completely cover the nail when plastering over the seams and nails before applying the paint.

Finish nails are naturally very thin and are designed to be not seen. Finish nails have a very thin head which is almost the same width as the nail itself. You want to use a small carpenter's hammer or ball ping hammer to drive finish nails into your work. Never use a power nailer for finish nails, because that power can make the nail go in too far. Along with your smaller hammers, you need a nail pin. The nail pin is designed to drive the finish the nail below the wood's surface. You can then use special putty to cover the nail and make it practically invisible. When putting finished wood as a vernier, you should use a combination of wood glue and finish nails for a stronger hold.

Screws come in a wide variety and sizes. The advantage of wood screws over nails is that screws can give a stronger hold than a nail. The threads of a screw can go deep enough and give a good grip on the wood where it will be very difficult to pry apart. Different types of screws are mentioned below.

Flat head screws are wood screws which have a flat head and typically have one slot across its head. These screws are the easiest to drive, especially if you have a power drill with a screw driver bit. The screw driver bit needed for flat head screws is a flat bit shaped like a spade. The flat part will fit into the slot on the screw's head.

Phillips screws are more difficult to drive in because of its special head. The common feature of a phillips screw is the drive slots on its head. Unlike a flat head screw, the Phillips screw has a cross for its drive slot. This means that you need a special Phillips screwdriver bit for your drill. Most drywall screws are Phillips screws.

Hex head screws are typically strong screws which are used to screw wood to concrete. Typically hex head screws are used when placing a floor plate or a wall stud when making rooms in a basement or on a slab for a single story home.

Properly Nailing and Screwing Pieces of Wood Together
When fastening wood together in many projects, you need to take some steps to keep the wood in tact. When building homes or additions to a home, you need to understand that most wooden planks, such as 2X4s, 2X6s, 2X8s, 2X10s, and 2X12s are made from pine. Pine is a good wood to work with but it is very knotty and has the potential to split or crack when you are trying to drive a nail or screw in. This means that you have to use care when fastening wood together.

We recommend that you drill pilot holes into the wood you want to drive a nail through. This is easy to do and the pilot hole should be narrower than the diameter of the nail. You may not necessarily need to do this when nailing 2X4s together for parts of a wall, but the harder the wood, the more likely it is to split. You need to keep this in mind. For example, if you want to nail oak base boards or other wooden pieces of a structure, drill the pilot holes.
Nailing finish nails should simply be done discretely. Typically, you don't need to drill pilot holes for finish nails, as they are very thin. You should use a strong wood glue along with the finish nails to ensure the trim holds.

Now that you know the basics, you need to see some of the projects we have in the next chapters.

Chapter Two

Simple Cabinet Making

Now that you know the basics of woodworking, you are ready to start on some projects. We want to start simple, so thus we want you to learn the simplest projects first. Here you will learn basic cabinetry or cabinet making. We always need good cabinets for small storage space, whether in the kitchen, bathroom, hobby room, or other places in your home. In this chapter, you will learn the following:

A. **Making a basic cabinet** which can be placed under the kitchen sink or countertop, under a workbench, or even the vanity in your bathroom.
B. **Adding shelves inside your cabinets** which are important, especially for overhead cabinets.
C. **Hanging overhead cabinets** in your kitchen, work room, sewing room, or other activity room in your home.
D. **Hanging cabinet doors and what hinges** can be used. In this segment, you will also be learning about locking mechanisms, especially magnetic locks, frequently used in most cabinets.
E. **Making glass cabinet doors** for cabinets which display collectibles, having fancy kitchen cabinets, etc.
F. **Cabinet lighting** for both cabinets with glass doors or lighting under overhead cabinet soffits: This segment will teach you lighting techniques which you can easily incorporate which eliminates the need for cumbersome and difficult to install can lights, unsightly fluorescent tubes, or other lights which stand out. You will learn how to create the perfect

accent lighting using puck lights, LED strips, and other small low voltage lighting systems which saves you money in both electrical cost and installation.
G. **Making a lazy Susan** which is referred to a corner cabinet which has a rotating set of shelves and are often found in most modern kitchens. The lazy Susan is a very practical cabinet which can store more than the typical conventional cabinet. A lazy Susan does not have to be limited to your kitchen, however. You can also use a lazy Susan in your hobby room or workshop to store small bottles of paints and finishes, tools, and more.

Making the Basic Cabinet
Making a basic cabinet is rather simple. Typically, these cabinets are designed to be placed under the kitchen sink and counter tops or can also be used as a vanity for your bathroom.

Dealing with plumbing can be an issue when building a cabinet which is to go under a kitchen or bathroom sink. Typically, when remodeling your kitchen or bathroom, you are likely to change the sink anyway, so it is a good idea to build this cabinet before you install the new sink. Basically, you will have to remove the drain pipe, which can be easily done. You will have to saw a hole in the back of the cabinet to accommodate the piping. See Figures One through Three to see how to work around the plumbing.

Figure One: The typical plumbing for a sink

Notice in Figure One above, you will have these basic piping to deal with any sink. The thicker pipe which has an S shape to it is the drain. This pipe is attached to the drain hole at the bottom of the basin of your sink. Some kitchen sinks may have two drains if they have a dual basin construction.

The two thin copper pipes are the feeds for your cold and hot water to your faucet. Inside the cabinet, you will notice that there is a valve which you can turn open or closed. You want to make sure the valves are completely closed before you remove any of these pipes, otherwise you will end up with a massive water leak. Sometimes, these valves are located in your basement or crawlspace. You will have to know where exactly all the rooms are in relation to your crawlspace or basement. Before you start any demolition and remove any plumbing, we recommend that you first find out which pipes are the correct ones, turn those valves to completely closed and test the faucet. If no water is coming from the faucet, then you closed the right valves. In some cases, if there is still some residual water left in the pipes, you will see some water running for a while, but you will see the flow stream become lesser in strength and then finally stop. Then you know it's safe to remove the pipes.

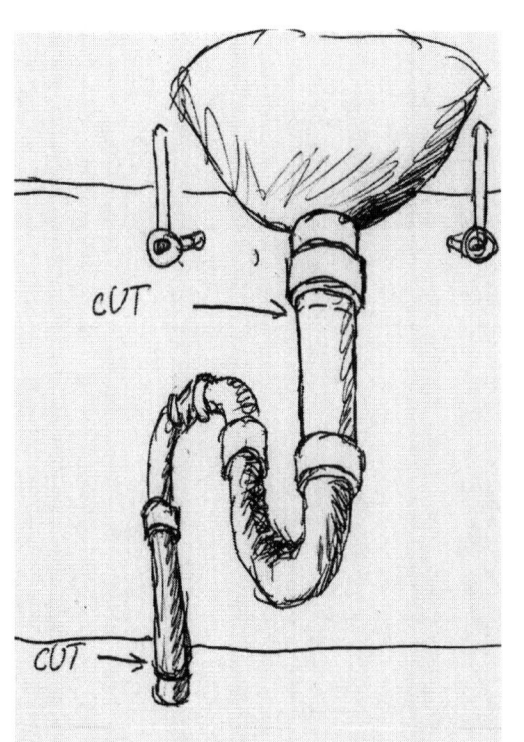

Figure Two: How to properly remove the drain pipe

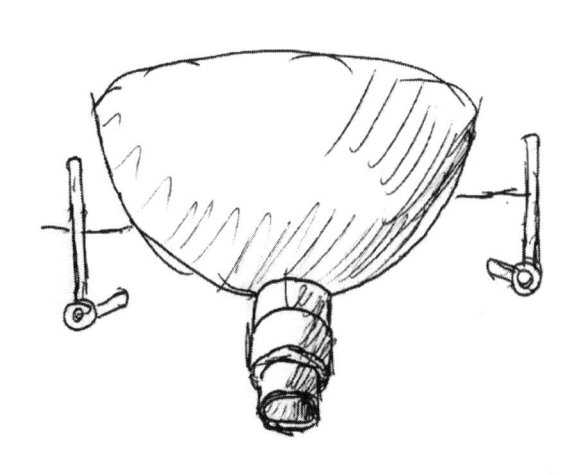

Figure 2a   Figure 2b

When removing the drain pipe, you want to use care while removing it first. Drain pipes can be very messy, especially if they are old and clogged. You want to make sure that the basin in your sink is not holding any water for a prolonged time. If this is your sink's description, then you want to make sure the water has trickled down until the basin is dry before attempting to remove the drain pipe.

Note, also when removing an old drain pipe, you can expect sludge to be coming out and this can be a messy job. Figure 2a shows you how to first remove the top of the drain pipe. This is the part that is connected to the drain of your sink. Figure 2b shows you how to remove the bottom of the drain pipe. This can go through either the bottom of the cabinet or elbows and goes through the bottom of the wall of the cabinet.

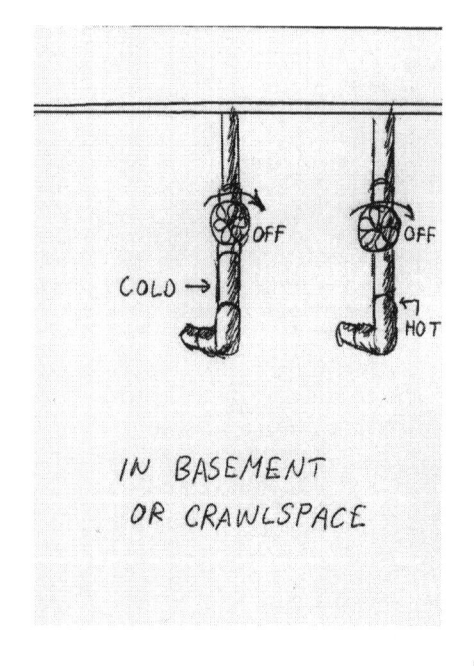

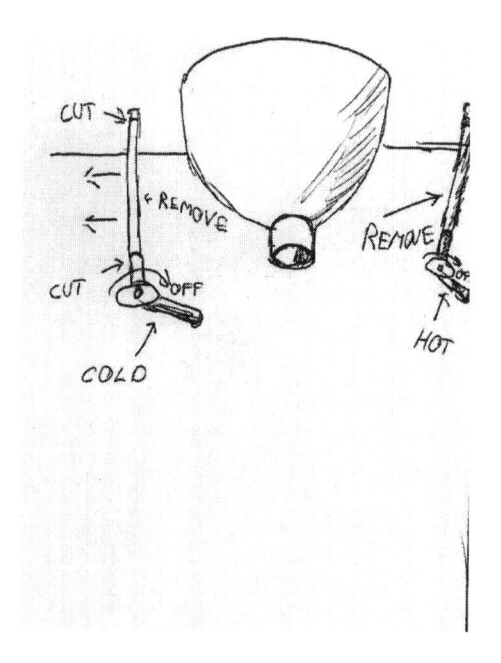

Figure Three: Removing the feed pipes to the faucet

Figure 3a   Figure 3b

Notice in the two figures above feed pipes to your sink's faucet can differ. Figure 3a shows the feed pipe connection with the valves directly under your sink. You will have to make the holes in the back wall of your cabinet have to be wide enough to pass through the valves and elbow joints of the pipes. Figure 3b shows the other variation which you frequently come across in other home constructions. This is where the feeder pipes come directly through the floor from the basement or crawlspace.

When you have this system, you are likely living in an older home and thus you will not only need to have the right holes in the cabinet floor, you will want to take some foam insulation and seal the holes around the pipes together with some steal wool or steel mosquito netting. The reason you want to have the steel wool or netting with the foam is to keep mice from chewing through the foam insulation.

Before you can start building your new cabinets, you should remove your old cabinets first and remove all the countertops and sinks. Once you have done this, you may want to have a rag which you can stuff into the drain pipe to keep sewage odors from coming up into the house.

Take measurements of your cabinets before removing them and then draw plans for the new cabinets. You will also want to measure the areas where all the pipes are so you can make sure you have the holes cut in the right spot of your new cabinet.

Building the basic case for your cabinets is the next step when building new cabinets. You want to remember, if you are building your cabinets which go under your kitchen countertop or a vanity for your bathroom, you will not need to make a top or cover for your cabinet. The counter top and sink is the top of your cabinet. Keep in mind that when making the cabinets under your sink, you should not plan to install drawers. The basin of the sink will take some space at the top of your cabinet. This is why classically, the cabinet under the kitchen sink often stores all the cleaning products.

In Figure Four below, you can see how the basic form of your cabinet should look like. This is the basic structure. Typically, the skeletal structure of a cabinet should be done with 2X2s. For lower kitchen cabinets and the vanity cabinet for your bathroom, you might want to think about using 2X4s as the corner posts since it has to support the weight of the sink and countertops. This especially holds true with granite or marble countertops, as natural stone is fairly heavy.

Figure Four: Basic skeletal structure for the lower cabinets.

When making the walls of the cabinets, you want to use fine wood instead of plywood for the visible parts of them. Good woods for cabinet making include pine, aspen, maple, mahogany, walnut, oak, or poplar. If you plan to carve patterns on the cabinet doors, you may want to have a softer wood, like aspen or basswood unless you are an experienced woodcarver. When carving, you should avoid using regular white pine, as this wood chips easily. Aspen is also a variety of pine, but it is a finer grain, thus it does not have the tendency to chip as much as regular white pine does. Mahogany is also a good wood to work with if you plan to carve patterns on the cabinets.

When building overhead cabinets, you basically follow the same design as mentioned above. With overhead cabinets, however, you want to use 2X2s or thinner lumber for the skeletal structure. These have to be hung to the wall with bolts, screws, and braces, thus they should be light enough for two or three people to hold the cabinets in place while they are being fastened to the wall.

Adding Shelves Inside your Cabinets
Having an organized kitchen, bathroom, or even workshop or hobby room requires organized cabinetry. Even pantries have shelves to store canned goods and other nonperishable foodstuffs. Thus, there is a need for making shelves in your cabinets. You need to think carefully when contemplating shelving for your cabinets, as it is very difficult, if not impossible to make adjustable shelves for the basic kitchen cabinet, so you want to make sure the shelves are the right height for the items you want to store.

Basic shelving for your kitchen cabinets is rather simple to make. First take measurements of the items to be stored in a particular cabinet. For example, if you are building a large pantry, you will want to measure all the cans you plan to store from the largest size ten cans to the smallest cans and make the shelves accordingly.

The lower kitchen cabinets will need drawers. Many kitchens have drawers to store flatware, knives, and other cooking utensils. This needs to be done in the basic skeletal structure of the cabinet and when you make the walls, you should set a structure which can support a slide rail on both sides to help open and close the drawer easily.

As seen in Figure Five below, you can see how simple it is to make shelving for the shelves inside your cabinet. Simply place two 2X2s, one on either side of the cabinet and temporarily nail them by not driving the nails in all the way. Make sure that they are level. You can check whether they are level by lying a board on them and checking them with a water level. Once you see they are level, screw them into place. Once the shelf supports are screwed in, you can either remove the nails or drive them in all the way. You should use nails which are smaller than 8 penny for cabinets.

Below in Figure Six, you can see how a slide rail can be placed for a cabinet drawer for your flatware, cooking utensils, and knives. You will be learning how to make drawers later on in this book.

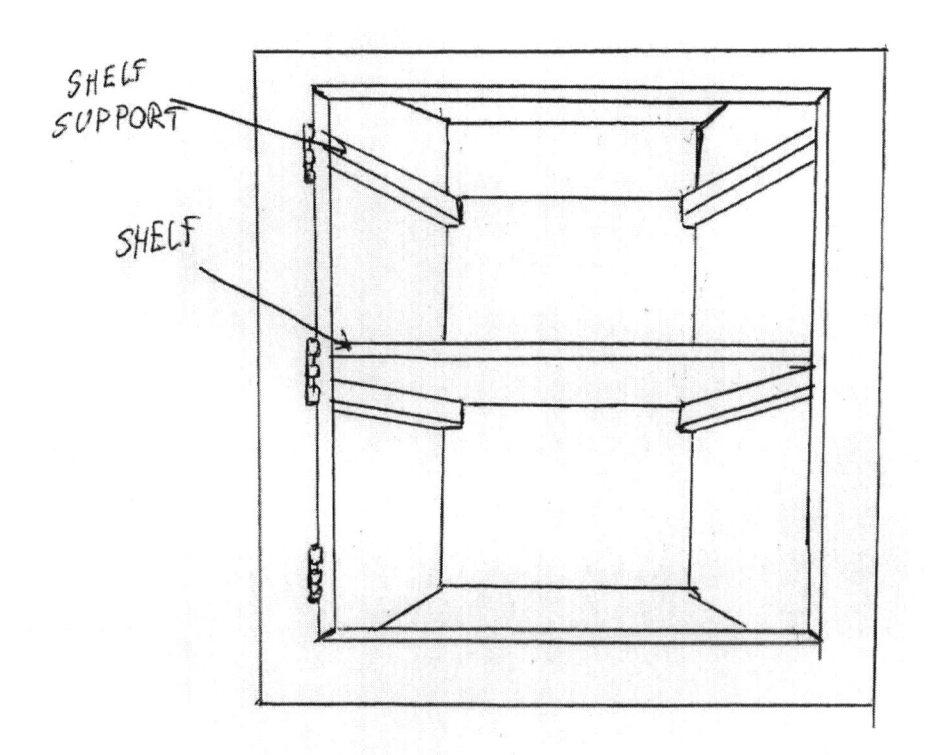

Figure Five: Setting the shelving inside your cabinets
Notice that in this cabinet, you have three shelves. Notice how you can use a water level to make sure the supports hold the shelf level before you drive in the final screws.

Some cabinets might have one or two shelves, depending on the size of the cabinet. You need to determine that according to your needs.

Figure Six: The slide rail for your kitchen drawers

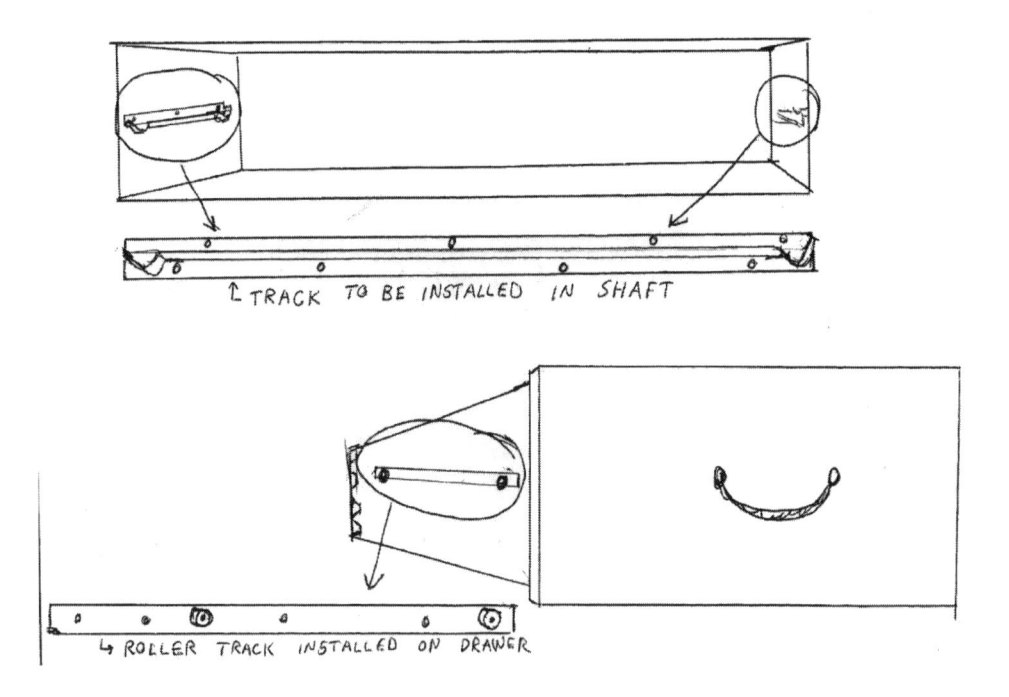

TRACK TO BE INSTALLED IN SHAFT

ROLLER TRACK INSTALLED ON DRAWER

Notice that the slide rail is basically a track which comes with small rollers which attach to the drawer itself. The rollers ride on the track and this allows you to open and close the drawer with ease.

Hanging Overhead Cabinets

The most difficult part of making kitchen cabinets is hanging them on the wall. There are many different ways you can hang the overhead cabinets, however, if you plan to use screws, you will need rather large and long wood screws and you will have to know exactly know where the studs are in the wall. Only wooden studs can support the weight of these cabinets with their contents. Just fastening them to the drywall will cause them to fall and rip out the drywall, leaving you with a mess in your kitchen.

Using braces is the ideal way to hang overhead cabinets to the wall. You can get a wide variety of braces for cabinets at any large home improvement chain, such as Menard's, Lowe's, or Home Depot. The one problem with braces, however, they can be unsightly so when installing them, you want to make sure they are installed in such a way they can be concealed with some sort of facade, such as tile, a granite or marble backsplash, or other decorative feature. Sometimes, you can even create a wooden broad trim with can also double as a lighting fixture.

Using braces is a much saver way to hang your cabinets, as they are stronger and are bolted into the studs and allow you to place the cabinet safely and not have to worry about the cabinets falling on your head when you are working in the kitchen. Seeing Figure Seven below, you can see the different kinds of braces which are available for hanging cabinets.

Figure Seven: See how you can use these braces to hang overhead cabinets.

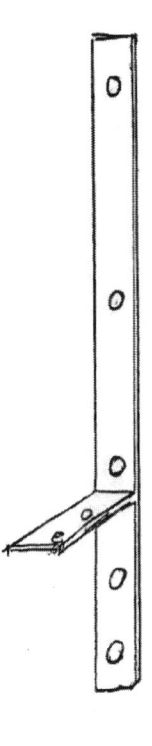

Notice that these kinds of braces can be found in almost any home improvement store. Hanging cabinets can be a dangerous job and it is not to be undertaken alone. You want to do this with two or three other people to help hang them securely.

Hanging Cabinet Doors with Hinges
Though there are some cabinet doors which are sliders, most kitchen cabinets and vanities in your bathrooms have hinged doors. There are many different kinds of hinges available which you can use to hang your doors. One thing that you will need along with hinges are magnetic locks to keep your cabinet doors closed.

Surface hinges are the simplest hinges to hang your cabinet doors with. These are hinges which screw directly on the front of the cabinet face and the front of the cabinet door. If you want to hang cabinet doors in this fashion, you will want to make sure they are decorative hinges, because some hinges which are designed for house doors can be plain and unsightly as they are designed to be attached to the inside of the doorframe and the side of the door.

You can see in Figures Eight and Nine below the different types of decorative hinges you can find. These are not all the styles available, but you can find more of them by browsing the internet or going to any Lowe's, Menard's, Home Depot, or any other large home improvement warehouse store.

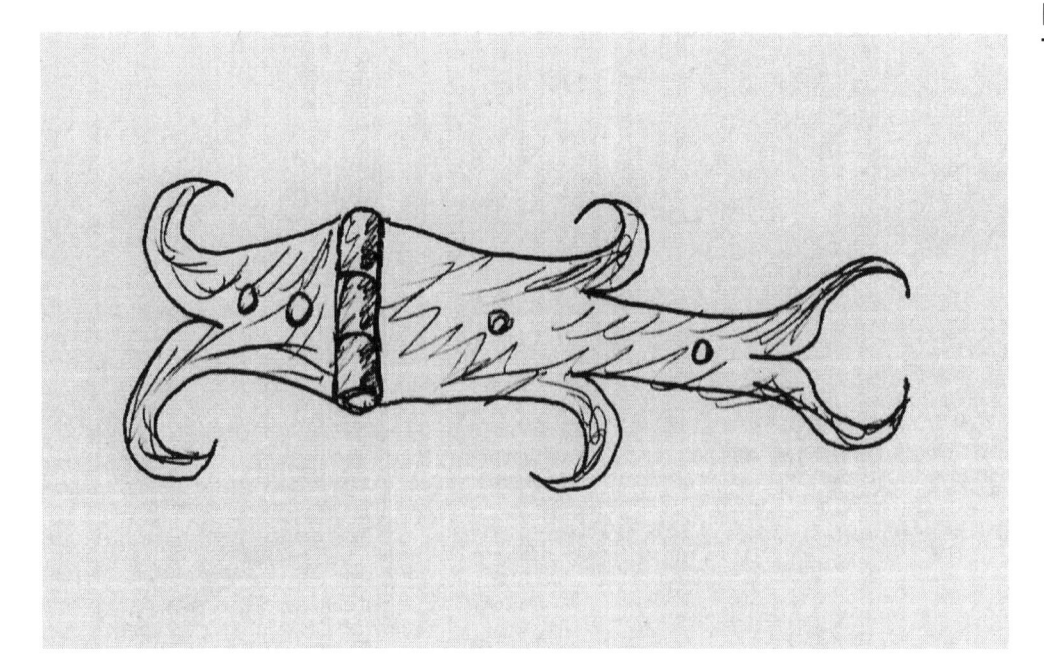

Figure Eight:
Tudor style hinges

Tudor style hinges are those which give that English Medieval look to your cabinetry. This style was often used in Tudor style homes which were home building kits offered by Sears after World War II. Many people who like to have the Tudor look will also stucco the outside of their homes and have leaded glass windows. If this is your style, these hinges would be ideal for you.

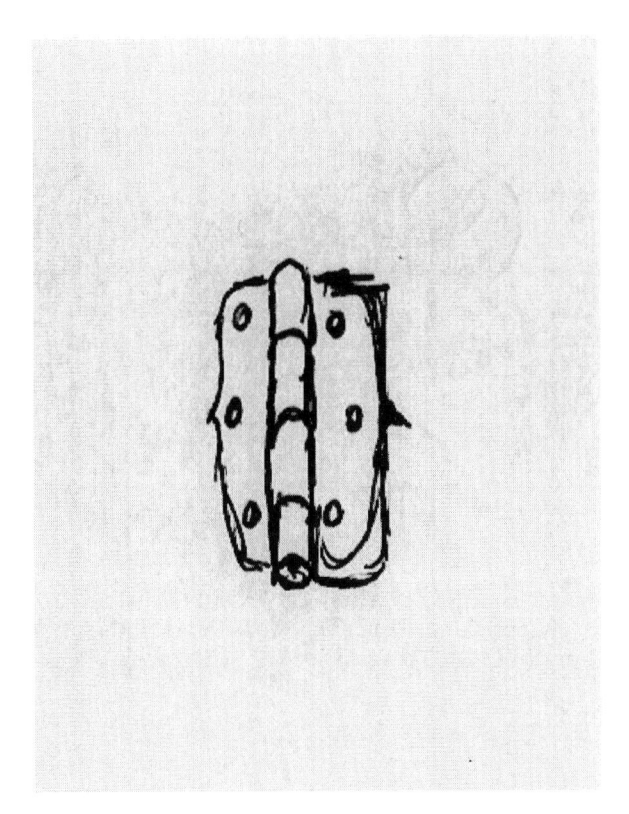

Figure Nine: Discrete and mildly decorative hinges

These hinges have some small decorative features to them and look nice, but they are also very modest. These are great for people who like a simple but sedate look to their kitchens.

Piano hinges are often used in cabinetry. A piano hinge is referred to a very long hinge which goes to most of the height of the cabinet door. Typically, piano hinges are used to attach the keyboard cover for pianos, hence the name. The nice thing about piano hinges is that the fastening panels of each side are rather narrow, so with the right cabinets, you can screw them to the side of the cabinet door and frame. This makes for one of the least visible hinges possible. A good illustration of a piano hinge is shown in Figure Ten below.

Corner hinges are an odd type of hinge. This hinge is designed to be discrete and one side is attached to the inside of the cabinet whereas the other side of the hinge is designed to be fastened to the door. Because these hinges can be difficult to install, the pivot pin can come out, so you can place the door on the workbench and screw on the hinge to the door and then the other half to the side of the cabinet. You can see this type of hinge in Figure Eleven below.

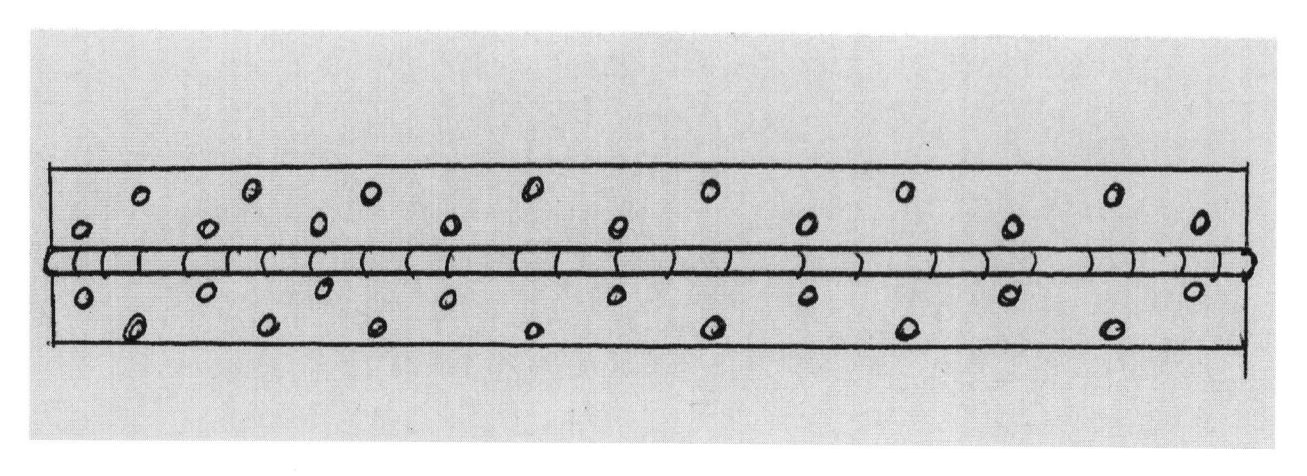

Figure Ten: The typical piano hinge

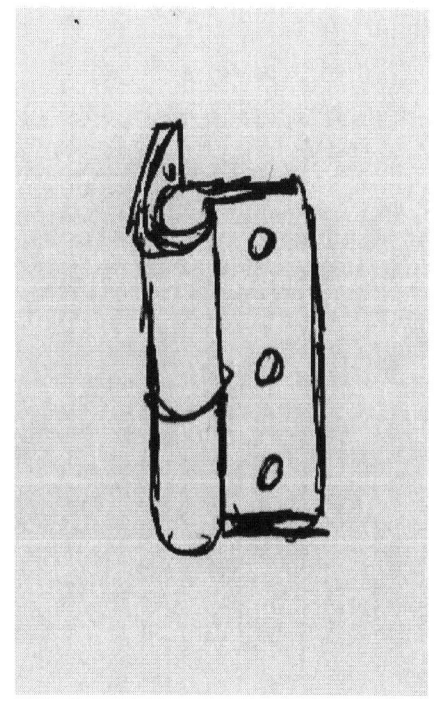

Figure Eleven: The typical corner hinge.

Making Glass Cabinet Doors
Sometimes you would like to have glass cabinets. This is quite understandable. You may have some fine china you want to proudly display. You may also have some fine silver serving sets or a gorgeous set of vintage CUTCO knives to show to your friends. Though these things are typically shown in as hutch in a dining room, you may have other reasons for glass cabinet doors in your kitchen. You can use transparent or translucent glass for your cabinet doors and have puck lights inside your cabinets for that special affect in your kitchen.

There are many ways you can incorporate glass in your cabinet doors. If you know how to do stained glass or leaded glass, this can be a great way to add beauty to your kitchen cabinets. The trick to attaching glass to your cabinet doors is so that it won't fall out. As far as leaded glass or stained glass, I'll leave that up to you, but what I will show you is how you can keep your glass work secure inside your cabinet door.

Making a glass door for your cabinets is by far more complicated than making a simple cabinet door out of solid wood. Tools you will need to make a glass cabinet door are listed below.

A. **A miter saw** is necessary as you will need to cut pieces of wood into 45 degree angles. This is so you can shape the door.
B. **Small carpenter's hammer** to gently nail the glass into the door.
C. **A router** to carve into the sides of what makes the door to hold the glass.

There are two different types of glass cabinet doors which you can fashion out of wood. One is simple and is deal for a single pain of glass and the other is for multiple smaller pains of glass. The latter is more complicated because most of the square pains have to be tediously placed in thin square slats of wood. They will both be explained and shown below.

The single pain cabinet door is very simple to make. Simply take your miter saw and cut a frame which will be the backbone of your door. You want to use planks of fine wood about two to three inches wide. Cut them to the right length and cut a 45 degree angle so you can connect the pieces to make a 90 degree angle.

Before you put the pieces of wood together to make the initial structure of the door, you want to use a router to carve out a groove along the inside side of the cabinet door. You want to measure the thickness of your glass. Also, when using these doors to have stained or leaded glass, the lead and glass together can be thicker than a normal single sheet of glass. You do not want the glass to be too loose, so you want to make sure that the lip is wide enough to snugly fit the glass. You don't want to make it too tight at the same time, because when you hammer, you could risk cracking or breaking the glass.

You want to fasten the glass to the cabinet door by taking a fastening strip which is a piece of thin, but strong wood which goes along the entire cabinet. Gently nail the wood beneath the lip you carved out with the router, being very careful not to break the glass. See Figure Twelve below how to install the glass in a cabinet door.

Figure Twelve: Installing the glass into your cabinet door.

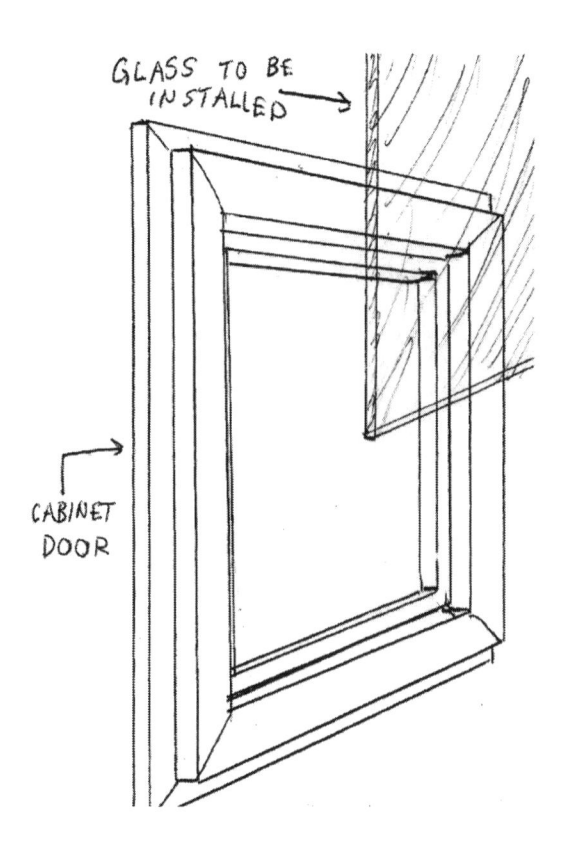

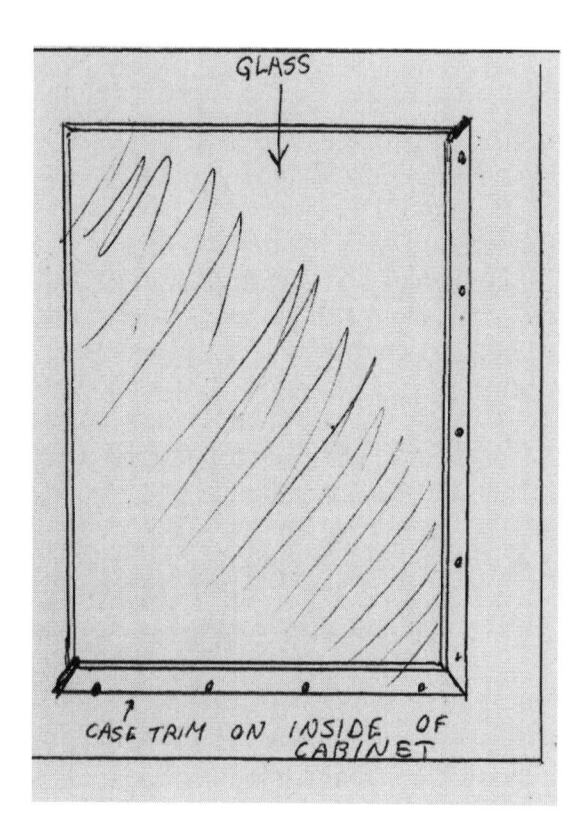

Figure 12a   Figure 12b

Notice that in Figure 12a, you can see the lip in the inside of the cabinet door in which the glass pain is being placed into. Figure 12b shows how to gently nail in place the wooden strip which will hold the glass into place so it cannot move out, fall, and shatter. Use care and hammer lightly, because any strong vibration can crack or break the glass.

Making a multiple pain cabinet door is much more complicated than making a single glass pain cabinet door. Basically, in this book we will show you how to add four pains in one door. This is much simpler and you can also do different styles, but the more glass pains you need to put into your door to accommodate your design, the more difficult it will be to make the door.

The first thing you will want to do when adding multiple glass pains to your door is to first take accurate measurements of the glass pains and then you will need to have strips of wood which are an inch thick on which you will need to carve a lip in with a router. You also want to carve a lip with your router like with a single pain door. You also want to carve a notch to add the dividers into the door. The dividers have to fit just right and be tight. Upon adding the glass, the smaller pains are much lighter than a single pain, so you should get a special wood putty which is known as mastic. This is a special putty which also works as a glue and allows you to glue the glass into the dividers. Mastic should be applied on the inside of the cabinet door. See Figure Thirteen below.

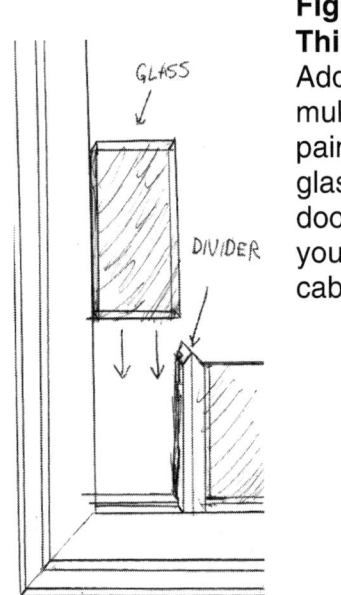

Figure Thirteen: Adding a multiple pain glass door to your cabinets

Figure 13a   Figure 13b   Figure 13c

Notice that in Figure 13a, you already have the cabinet door ready to add the glass. In Figure 13b, you can see how the glass is placed into each square. Sometimes, you may want to take some short finish nails to toe nail into the lip of the door and dividers. Do this very carefully and use a nail driver with the hammer do you don't risk hitting the glass with your hammer. The small nails will help keep the glass in place and then Figure 13c shows how the mastic should be applied. The mastic together with the nails will give the glass the hold it needs to stay in its place.

Our advice when wanting to make glass cabinet doors is to have several extra pains of glass cut for your doors. Especially if you are a beginner. It's not even uncommon for professional cabinet makers to break glass when trying to install it into a cabinet door. The spare will allow you to finish your project in due time.

Cabinet Lighting
Now that all your cabinets are in place, you want to have a kitchen you can show off to your friends and neighbors. It's time to think about good lighting. You want lighting which will give you ample lighting when working in the kitchen, yet at the same time, you want to have lighting that looks good and professional. There are all kinds of lighting options you can use, but we will cover the most common ones here.
Puck lighting is the easiest lighting to install. One of the reasons why puck lighting is so easy to install is because you don't have to be a certified electrician to do it. There is little or no wiring involved and you only need to plug it into a regular wall outlet and you are ready to go. Puck lights are lights which can be either LED, Xenon bulb, or halogen lighting. They are low voltage and are connected to a wire which can be stapled to the bottom of your overhead cabinets soffits. The Xenon lights are better than the halogen lights, because they give as much light as a halogen light, but the Xenon gas bulbs do not burn as hot as halogen bulbs. Furthermore, you can handle Xenon bulbs with your bare hands, unlike halogen bulbs which can burn out easily if the oils from your hands get on the bulb.

Typically, puck lights have a harness which can be glued to the cabinets soffits with a good epoxy glue and the puck lights lock into place. These light fixtures are called puck lights because they look like and are about the size of a hockey puck.

LED strips are becoming very popular because they are so easy to install and do not take much electricity. LED lights are becoming much brighter than they were just ten years ago. LED strips can simply be glued onto the bottom of your cabinets soffits or on the side wall. Like puck lights, they are usually attached to a wire which you can plug into a wall outlet.

Making a Lazy Susan
Having a lazy Susan in your kitchen is very convenient. They can be a bit tricky to build, but it's doable. Making a lazy Susan is basically making a circular set of shelves which are fastened to a corner door which pivots around. The whole idea of a lazy Susan is so that you can spin the shelves in a cabinet to reach something. These are ideal for those kitchen cabinets in the corner.

Building the axel on which the lazy Susan pivots on is the most difficult part of this cabinet. You should already have the skeletal structure build as you were making all your other cabinets and installing the countertops. The best way to have the axel work is a wooden dowel rod which can be attached to two free spinning gyros which can be found in most hardware stores.

Building the door to fit into the corner can be done by fitting the two wood panels to the dowel rod with some special metal fasteners. At the same time, you will want to make the shelves in a circular shape with one quarter cut out. This is where the door panels are placed. Build this all around the axel and you're set.

Cabinet making is a big undertaking and if you want to remodel your house, this is something you need to learn.

Chapter Three

Shelving

Shelving is something that is highly needed in many households. Shelving is the most common and the easiest storage method to build in your closets, bathrooms, kitchens, workshops, and other places where shelves are needed. In this chapter you will learn how to make a whole variety of different shelves for the simple heavy duty shelves for your garage, shed, or workshop to elegant fancy shelves which you can use as bookcases and shelves for trinkets in your study, den, living room, or reading nook. In this chapter you will learn to make both adjustable and fixed shelves and it will be broken down from the simplest to the most complicated as listed below.

A. **Heavy duty shelves** which is solely designed for functionality. These shelves are not intended to be decorative and are designed to hold heavy items, such as power tools, car items, gardening tools, and other basic things you can expect to find in your garage, shed, workshop, or basement.
B. **Permanent shelving** which can be both adjustable and fixed. In this segment, you will learn how to make these shelves to be fixed and you will also learn how to make adjustable shelves and how to install shelving strips with inserts which can hold a shelf. These shelves are designed to be both decorative and functional. These shelves can be used for books, photo albums, and trinkets you have acquired on your vacations.
C. **Decorative wall shelves** which are primarily used as a shelf in the kitchen for cookbooks, or can also be used as decorative ornamentation and hold trinkets, collectibles, and other nicknacks you acquire, souvenirs from that special vacation, etc.
D. **Movable shelves and bookcases** which are basically shelves in a furniture unit. This is actually a piece of furniture and primarily intended to hold books. You can store almost anything with these shelves, but they are movable, so this project is ideal for those of you who tend to rent or like to move a lot.

Heavy Duty Shelves

If you are a handyman and like to do things with your hands, you will need these kinds of shelves. These shelves are ideal for the garage, the shed, workshop, or any area where decoration is not paid attention to.

The purpose of heavy duty shelves is for hard core storage. These shelves are made to be strong and if properly constructed, they can hold things as heavy as car jacks, suitcases, gas powered tools, such as chainsaws, weed eaters, leaf blowers, and more. Typically, they are made from the cheapest materials used in home construction, such as 2X4s and 2X6s and heavy duty plywood or particle board.

Building heavy duty shelves is very simple to do. Basically, you want to gauge what kind of weight you want to put on these shelves. If they are designed to hold heavy items, such as backpack leaf blowers, car jacks, chainsaws, suitcases, trunks, and things of the like, you may want to consider using 2X6s or in some cases, you may even want to think about using 2X8s. You also need to remember that you should also know how heavy things are and are you able to lift these items high enough to make it on the shelf. When thinking about that, the heavier items should be stored on the lower shelves and the lighter items should be stored on the higher shelves.

The best idea for a heavy duty storage shelving project for your garage, shed, or workshop is shown below in Figure One.

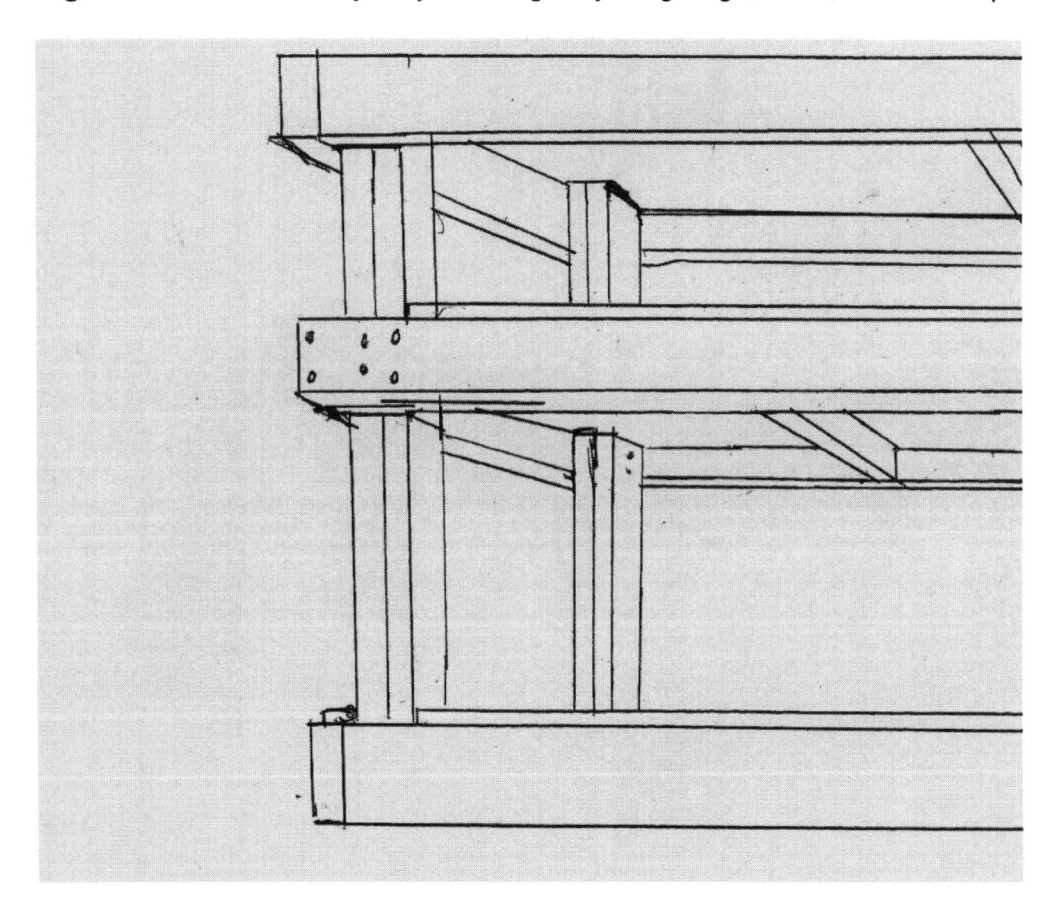

Figure One: Ideal heavy duty shelving for your garage, shed, or workshop

Notice that in Figure One above, the lower shelves have more space between them than the higher shelves. There is a reason for this kind of planning. Basically, most people, as they get older, have more difficulty lifting heavier items higher. When building your shelves, you want to think long term and have the heavier items stored on the lower shelves. Likewise, some items which are large and an awkward shape can be difficult to lift up, even if they are fairly light weight. A good example of this are suitcases. Most empty suitcases are fairly light, especially the newer ones, as they are made from lighter materials. You want to be able to comfortable accessing your suitcases, then you should place them on the shelf which you can easily place them on when not in use and easily remove them when you are packing them to go somewhere. You want to remember that if you feel like you are about to take your back out, then you are trying to place the item up too high for its weight.

Planning is the most important part of building your heavy duty shelves. You need to make accurate plans for this project. Basically, the steps that you can take make a good plan for your project is to take measurements. The keys to taking measurements are mentioned below.

A. **Measure** the area where you want to build your shelves. We actually recommend that you first take measurements of your area. For example, if these shelves are for your garage, you want to take measurements of your garage, measure how much space you will have between the shelves and your car. Likewise, if you are building your shelves in your basement, you need to take measurements of your basement or the room in your basement which you have kept as a storage room. Once you have the dimensions of the area where the shelves are to be built, then you don't need to worry about turning that area into an obstacle course when you are actually building them.

B. **Know what you are planning to store** before attempting to build the shelves. The best way to do this is to take measurements of the items you want to store. This is easily done with more fixed shaped items, which are either squares, rectangles, or circles, such as suitcases, power tool cases, boxes, filing drawers, etc. These are the easiest items to take measurements of and get the dimensions of. Other items which have a more organic shape, such as many power tools, backpack and hand-held leaf blowers, chainsaws, weed eaters, and like items, you want to measure from the lowest point to the highest point as well as the length of the item. This should give you a better inkling of how big you need to build your shelves. You want to make sure that when planning the space between shelves, you want to have at leave at least five inches below the upper shelf to allow for easy movement of that item on that shelf.

C. **Use of the right wood** for construction to make the shelves is also important. 2X4s are good for most items, but for heavier items, you need something stronger. If you are planning to store Heavy items, you need to build your shelves with 2X6s and then use a good three-quarter inch thick plywood or particle board, which is what is used for floors. Our advice is that the lower shelves which generally hold the heavier items be made with the stronger 2X6s and then the upper shelves, which will typically hold the lighter stuff and can be easily lifted over your head be made with 2X4s.

The perfect shelving structure for heavy duty storage shelves is best shown in the photograph shown below in Figure Two. As you notice in the photograph in Figure Two, the shelves did not really have the idea of having the lighter items on the bottom in mind, but we chose to photograph these shelves because they were well constructed and is a perfect example how 2X6s are used to make the shelves sturdy enough to hold a wide array of file boxes, suitcases, and more.

Figure Two: The typical heavy duty storage shelving built in a basement

Notice how these shelves are built. The shelves are very sturdy and are capable of holding the heavy items which are sitting on them. The important thing to notice here, when building these shelves, nails are not used. Nails simply won't support weight in such a small area. You are better off using eight penny wood screws.

Screws should always be used when fastening the 2X6s together, as shown above in Figure Two. These screws which are used in the shelves shown above are eight penny brass self drilling phillips wood screws. These screws are ideal as they have threads which are also like an auger and are designed to dig into the wood and can be driven in with a normal power drill which is outfitted with a phillips screwdriver bit.

Support for the shelves which are illustrated in the photos shown in Figure Three below are also very simple to do. We would even advise using an extra 2X6 to double the 2X6 making the vertical post for extra support on the shelves to ensure that they can support the weight you expect them to hold.

Figure Three: The two types of corner supports for the construction of the shelves shown in Figure Two.

Figure 3a   Figure 3b

Notice that the storage shelves featured in that basement first shown in Figure Two are rather complicated. Some of the shelves are wider than others to store certain different things. Figure 3a shows a suspended support which is a 2X4 which the bottom of is screwed to the 2X6 frame of the shelf and the top of is screwed to the floor joist of the floor of the room above. You also notice in Figure 3a, there is a continuation of the shelf which does not jet out. This is supported with standard floor post made from a 2X6 to give that extra support so the shelf can hold the suitcases and file boxes. The suspended support only works in a situation which is shown in Figure 3a.

In Figure 3b, you see the standard way of fastening the shelf to the corner post. The frame of the shelf is screwed to the 2X6 with the driver screws mentioned above. Notice that at the corner underneath the plywood, you can see that there is a double 2X6 used for extra support. This is crucial, as these shelves are designed to hold a large amount of weight long term. You need to have a strong enough support all that weight.

Basic shelf construction is rather simple to do. To build a setup as shown above in Figures Two and Three, you will need to follow some of the simple steps below.

A. **Prepare the 2X6s** and cut them down to size after taking measurements. If you ever have watched This Old House on PBS with Bob Vila back in the day, you probably have heard the saying which both Bob Vila and Norm Abram would say: Measure twice, cut once. That is very true with any of these projects in this book, especially this one. You need to remember, you can always remove more, but you can't put anything back. Measure the height of the walls and the width of the shelves. Then once you are certain about the measurements, you can go ahead and cut the pieces.
B. **Prepare the support posts against the wall first** before you begin building the horizontal parts of the shelves. You also need to understand the environment of the shelves being build. If you are building them in your basement, you probably have either concrete or cinder block walls to deal with. If your basement walls are made from poured concrete, you have an even harder surface to nail the support 2X6s to. Use concrete nails or screws when fastening these supports in. If you are building the shelves in your shed, workshop, or garage, and you have a typical stud and plate construction wall, then simply nail some horizontal 2X6s to the studs and screw the supports to those.
C. **Build the frame for the bottom shelf first** and use a water level to make sure everything is level. Some older homes might have a floor which is uneven, thus you can always make the first shelf level by placing shims underneath the initial 2X6s as seen in Figure Four below. Those of you who are building these shelves on a concrete floor of an outdoor shed, it is a good idea to have a wood shelf on the bottom to keep moisture from items you are storing. This is especially true if you store mortar or concrete mix bags, which can be ruined if they sit on the bare cement and moisture creeps up and through the paper of the bag.
D. **Upon completing the frame of the first and bottom shelf,** you can then begin to install the 2X6s which go vertical on the front part of the shelves. When installing the front support posts, you want to use your water level to check if they are plum (See Figure Five below). Use a single temporary nail not driven all the way in so you can move the post until plum. You may want to have someone help you with this part of the project so you can hold the horizontal pieces in place until they are level or to fasten them temporarily.
E. **Construct the frame for each individual shelf** from bottom upward. It should take the second shelf to make the front support posts plum. Build each shelf frame as shown in Figure Six below.

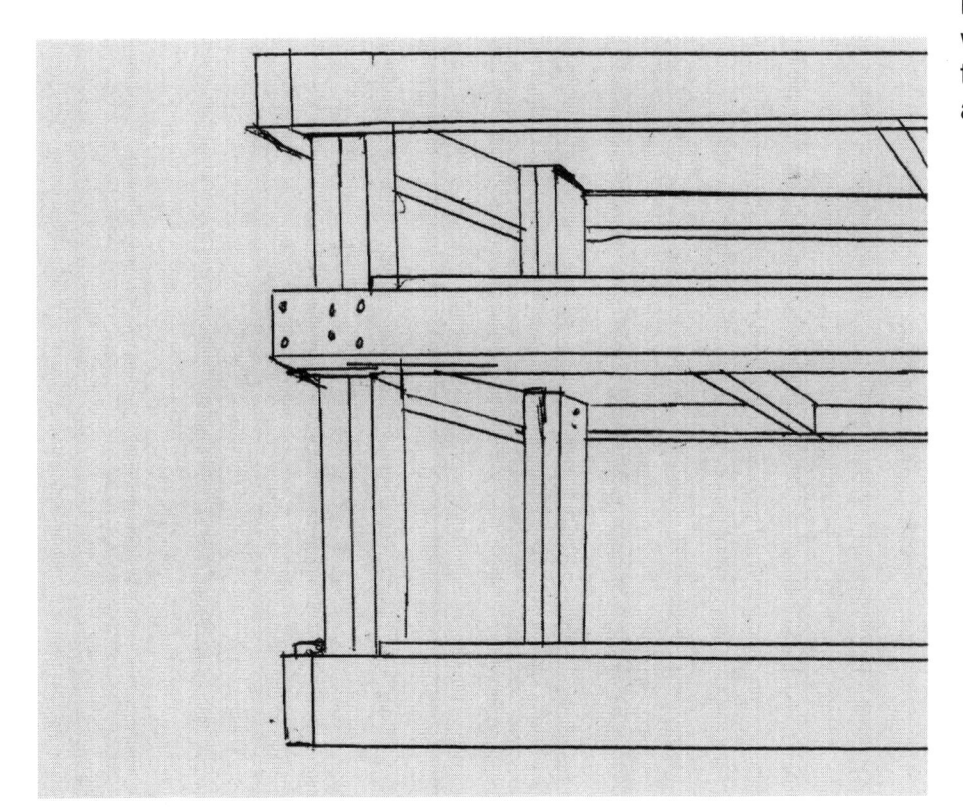

Figure Four: Using a water level to check how the 2X6s are both plum and level

Notice in Figure Four, the level is held up against the vertical support post and the air bubble in the water of the top glass tube is between the two lines on the tube. This is how the water level should look when plum.

In Figure Five, you can see how the 2X6, which is horizontal, is level by the middle water tube has the air bubble in between the two lines. Once you see everything is plum and level, then you can start screwing everything back together. One caveat, however, when you see the post is plum, place a second temporary nail to keep it from moving. Once you see that the horizontal 2X6 is level, then nail the other end. It should stay, then you can screw it in and remove the nails. Repeat the process for each shelf.

As you have completed the framework of the shelves, it's time to put the plywood in place. This can easily be done by cutting sheets of plywood to fit over the shelf frame. When constructing the framework for the shelves, you may want to have some 2X6s at every 12 to 24 inch interval to add extra support. Furthermore, this will make it easier to nail the plywood and allows you room for seems when a sheet of plywood does not cover the entire shelf. See Figure Five below.

Figure Five: How the shelf framework should look like before you lay the plywood.

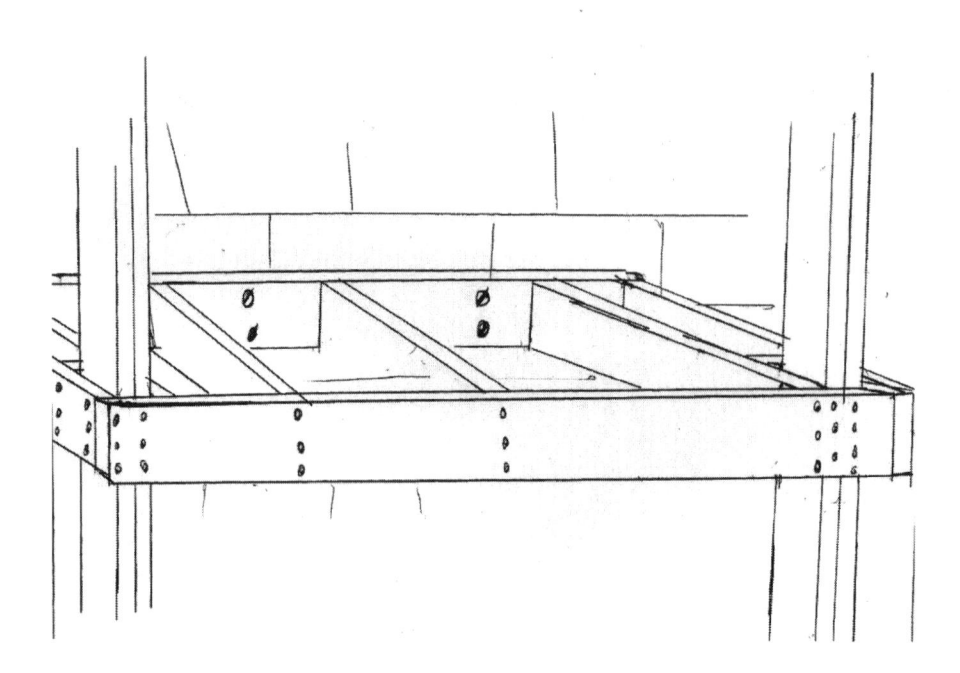

Notice that in Figure Six above, you can see that the 2X6s are put in at every even interval, which can be 12 to 24, which is recommended. The heavier the stuff you want to store is, then use smaller intervals for support beams.

Permanent Shelving
Permanent shelving is basically shelving you have incorporated in any room of your home and can be adjustable or fixed. The need for permanent shelving can differ from household to household. Unlike the heavy duty shelving we covered above, which is also permanent shelving, this shelving is different. Unlike the heavy duty shelving you have for your garage, shed, basement, or workshop, this permanent shelving is designed for it to be visible. Basically, it's not really designed to hold heavy objects, but more books, souvenirs, or other trinkets and collectables you want to show off to guests or anyone else invited to your home.

Building permanent shelving is best to do so it is recessed in the walls. If you are remodeling a home and there is no place to recess the shelves in the walls, then you need to study the floor plan closely and make a decision how you want to place the shelves so they are recessed in the walls. Sometimes, there might be a closet in a useless place. You can simply close up the closet and break out the wall and build a wall in the middle of the closet. Then you have permanent shelving in two rooms. Other rooms might have an irregular shape and have a notch where you can't put any furniture. This can be a great place for a set of permanent shelves.

Corner shelves are another great way to have permanent shelves in your home. Corner shelves are ideal for those of you who have small houses and have limited storage space. The great thing about corner shelves is that they can be ideal for showing off collectables, trinkets, photos, and more.

When building your permanent shelves whether recessed in the wall or going the entire parallel of the wall to the doorway is very simple to do. Ideally, you will want to have an open doorway going into your room and esthetically, if you have an arched doorway, you do not want the shelves to but up to the door. Another idea, if you love to collect things or have lots of books, you can also do a whole wall in shelving and even have shelves go above the door. Some private libraries also have a mobile step ladder which is guided on top by a track to help you reach the higher shelves. This can be a neat idea and allow for a subject of conversation for your guests. These projects will be covered in more depth in this segment below.

Building corner shelves is a fairly easy project to get involved in. Basically, you can have straight shelves which would be cut in a perfect triangle and the front of the shelves would be completely straight. This is ideal for trinkets, collectables, or souvenirs, but not the greatest for books. If you want to have a corner shelf for books, you want to have round shelves which you can arrange the books along the edge and make wooden wedges as book ends on either side. Seeing what shapes the two shelves should be cut is illustrated in the images below in Figure Six below.

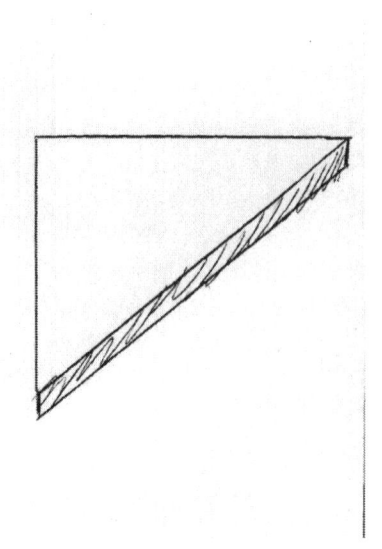

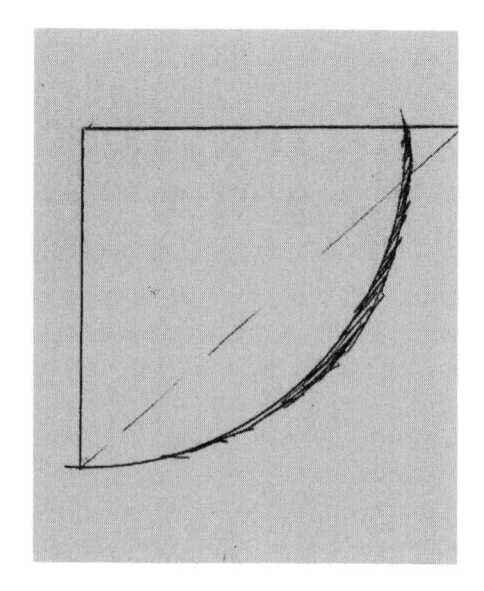

Figure Six: How wooden planks should be cut for a simple corner shelf construction.

Figure 6a   Figure 6b

Notice that in Figure 6a, the shelves will be straight and at a diagonal from the point of the corner. These shelves are to be cut in a perfect triangle with a right angle at one corner and two 45 degree angles on the other two corners, this way it will fit beautiful into the corner.

In contrast, Figure 6b shows the rounder shelf. This one has a right angle at the end which is supposed to but up to the corner, and the outer edge is round, like a semicircle. This can allow you to display a book, CD, or DVD collection.

Installing the shelves is also not too difficult to do. You first have to decide whether the shelves will be set in permanently and not able to move or do you want them movable incase you need to adjust the height in the future. This is something to think about. If you are building a corner shelf for your trinkets, collectables, or souvenirs and you are constantly traveling to exotic places, you will want to think about having the ability to move the positioning of the shelves. Ideally, you want to have two inches of space between the very top of the objects you are placing on these shelves and the bottom of the next shelf.
Installing fixed shelves is rather simple. Basically, if you like to have wall exposed, this method is the best, as long as you know where the stud work is in the house. You can, however, purchase a stud detector at any of the big home improvement stores, such as Menard's, Lowe's, or Home Depot. A stud detector basically is a small hand held metal detector and it also has a laser accurate system to sense the presence of nails or screws in a vertical manner. This is how it finds the studs and you don't have to tear out any drywall.

Simply take a small pice of 2X2 or even a 1X1 and cut to length of shelf. If you prefer 1X1s, you might have to buy 1X2s which are typically used as furring strips to nail wood paneling to concrete walls. You will have to use your table saw to rip them in half then you have two 1X1s which you can use as shelf supports. You can see how to install the shelves below in Figure Seven.

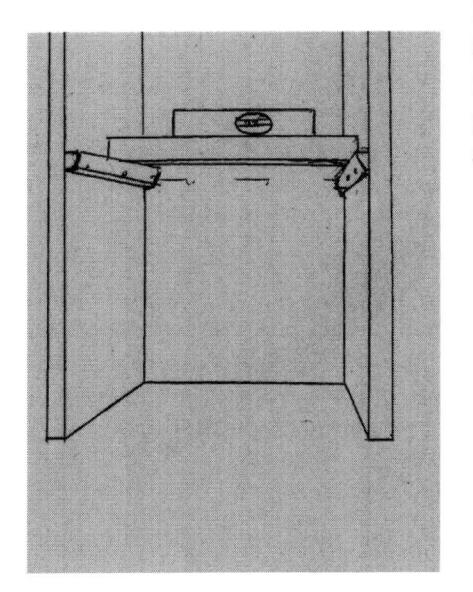

Figure Seven: Installation of a permanently fixed shelf

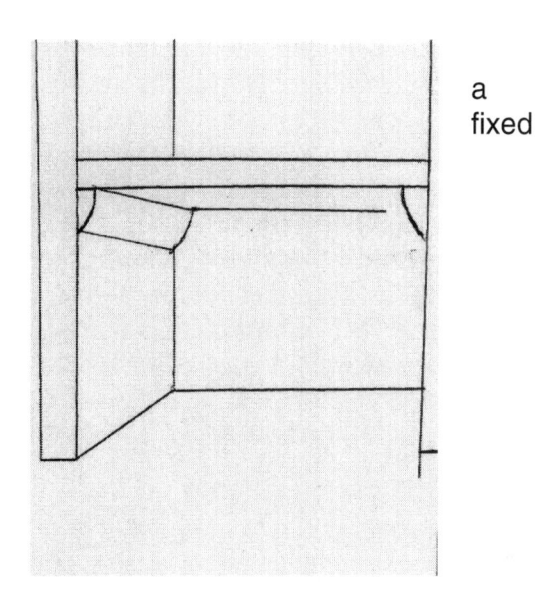

Figure 7a   Figure 7b

Notice that in Figure 7a, you can see that the shelf support is nailed into the wall with finish nails. Basically, these kinds of shelves are designed to hold things which are typically light weight, such as small collectables, possibly decorative or antique bottles, miniature cars, souvenir trinkets, such as little things which represent the ethnicity of a particular country you visited, and so on. If you are planning to use these shelves for books, then you should use 2X2s instead of 1X2s as they can be heavier. Notice that in Figure 7a, you can also see that a small water level is used to check that the shelf support is level. This is very important, because if the supports are not level, then the shelf won't be level.

If Figure 7b, you can see that the shelf is placed right on top of the two supports and is nailed into place with finish nails. Basically, when using finish nails, you want to think about using a strong adhesive to glue the supports to the wall. This is important as finish nails are rather thin and the shelf can simply be nailed down to the supports without use of adhesive.

Setting up corner shelves which can be adjusted can be a bit more complicated, but doesn't have to be. There is a rather large demand for shelving and hardware for shelves, so you can go to any home improvement store and get special tracks with notches which have pegs which lock into the notches and support the shelves. The trick is that you need to make sure that the notches are level with each other. These tracks are simple to install also. They simply screw into the wood. The one thing that differs when building a permanent set of adjustable shelves, you need to have some wood paneling the width of the shelves that go from floor to ceiling, or desired height.

Before installing the wood paneling, you will need to use a router and a guide fence to carve a straight groove into the wood which is the depth of the shelving track you plan to screw into the wood. Once you have installed the panels on either side of the corner, then you can install the shelving tracks. You should have two tracks per panel. This will ensure the shelf has ample support for the shelf and what it is supposed to hold.

When installing the shelving tracks, you want to have one or two people help you and hold them into place so you can take two of the shelving pegs and double check that the notches are level with each other. Shelving tracks are typically factory made, so if one set of shelving pegs is level, they all will be level. You can see in Figures Eight and Nine below how shelving track should be installed.

Figure Eight: After wood panel is installed into corner, simply place the shelving tracks into groove and check with water level to see if shelf will be level. Then screw them in.

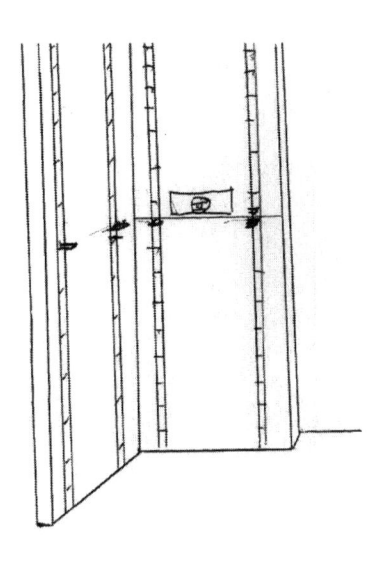

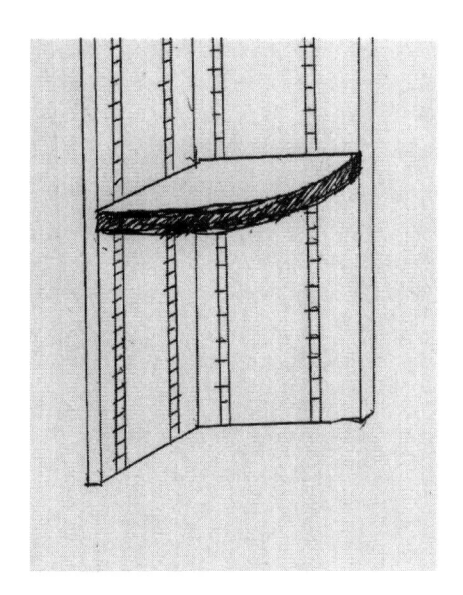

Figure 8a

Figure 8b

Notice in Figure 8a how the shelving tracks are first placed into the grooves in the wood panel and then a water level is used to check if the pegs are level with each other.

Figure 8b shows how you repeat the process in Figure 8a, but this time, have a trapezoid piece of wood which can fit on the outside. Place the water level on top of it to check if the pegs on both panels are level with each other. If they are, then screw in the tracks on the other side and you are able to place the shelf where you would like.

Figure Nine: The finished product

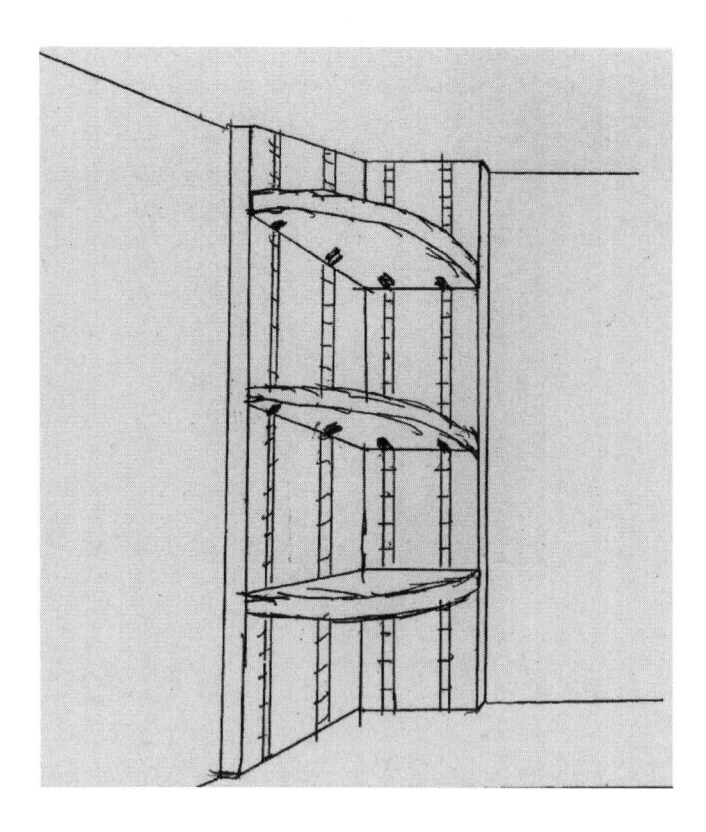

Notice in Figure Nine above, you can see how your corner shelves will look when finished. The shelves portrayed in Figure Nine are the simpler straight corner shelves. When it comes to the round shelves and you want to use them for books, then you can get creative with book ends. You can use wood for them or you can also use stones or other objects which can wedge in the gap between the wall and the book. This way your books will stay in proper place. Corner shelves can be difficult for books as the sides of the end books will not but right up against the walls as the corner shelf poses different angles from the wall and the sides of the books.

Floor to ceiling wall shelving is ideal for your private library, office, or den. Actually, you can also have floor to ceiling shelves in your living or dining room, especially if it has an adjacent reading nook in it. What will make this even more interesting is that you can have a movable stepping stool which is guided by a track at the top of the shelves and can move along the whole length of the shelves allowing you easy access to your books, regardless how high they are stored.

To begin, you want to draw a layout for your shelves. Ideally, you want your shelves to be built into a wall where there are no doors or windows. If there is a doorway, you should either remove the door or make sure it swings open outward, not into the room. The shelves could hinder the opening and closing of the door if it swings into the room. If you have to have a door that closes and the wall with the door is the only wall where you can have the bookshelves, then a sliding pocket door is the best option. You will learn how to make pocket doors later in this book.

Basically, the ideal way to build the shelves are as follows.

A. **Build the vertical supports** for the shelves. Use fine wood as you do not need to make thick walls for these shelves. You want these shelves to look nice, so you want to use a fine wood. At the bottom and top of the support boards, you will want to add some extra pieces of wood so that the walls can stand freely. Be sure to have the grooves carved into the wood if you want shelving track for adjustable shelves.
B. **The lower shelf** should be permanent and you can then cover the bottom with a baseboard to make it look like it is a permanent fixture of the room.
C. **Build a crown** at the top of the shelves beneath the ceiling. You will also want to get a banister which goes the entire length of the shelving unit. You can then install the hardware for the movable step and place the rail at the top of the shelving unit.

See how this can be done in Figures Ten Through Twelve below.

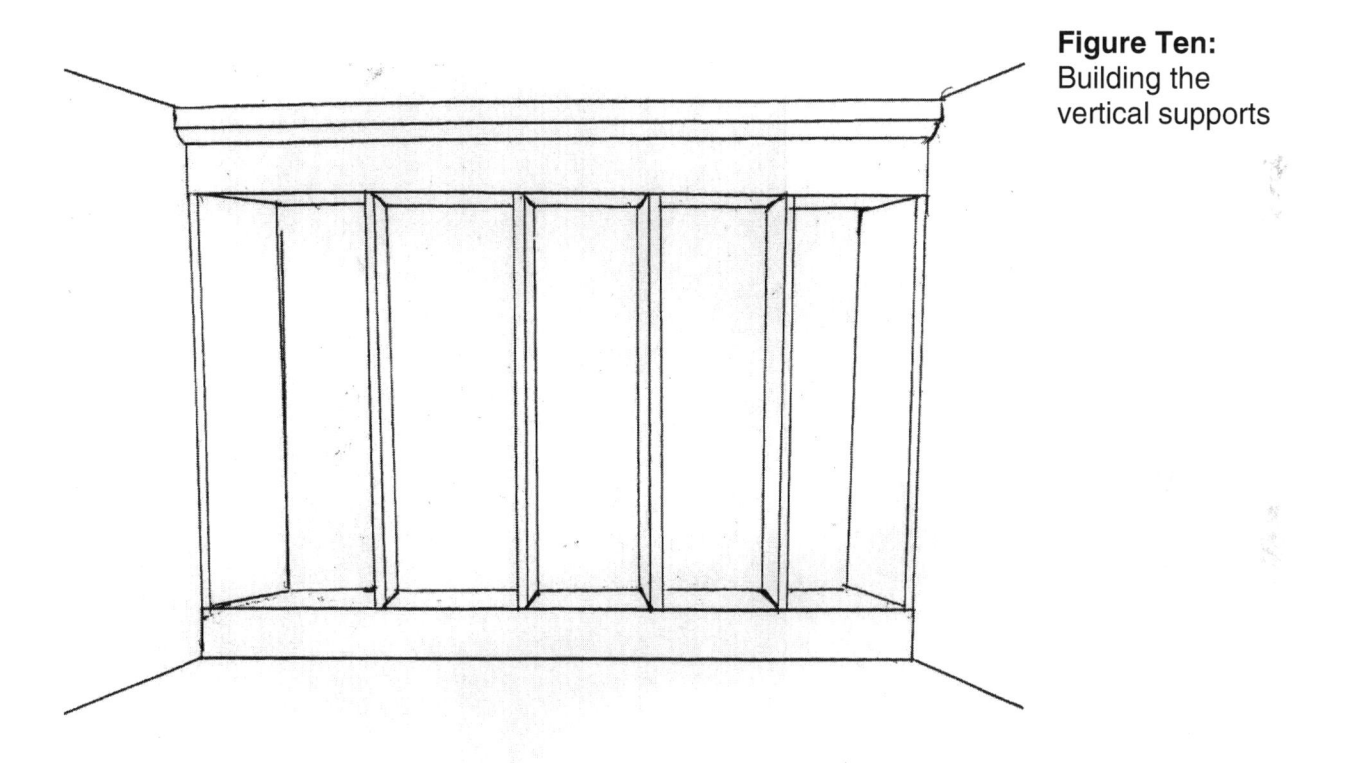

Figure Ten: Building the vertical supports

Notice that when building the vertical supports, you simply need a 2X4 on each side of the support, as they will be covered up by the bottom shelf and with the baseboard covering the two 2X4s on the bottom. Likewise, the crown molding and the board covering the top above the top shelf will cover the 2X4s on the top of the vertical supports. When placing the upper supports, pay attention to see where the ceiling joists are. You can use a stud detector to do that as well.

My advice is to screw into place a couple of 1X2s in the ceiling and then place the supports for your shelves.

Figure Eleven: The guide rail for the mobile stepper

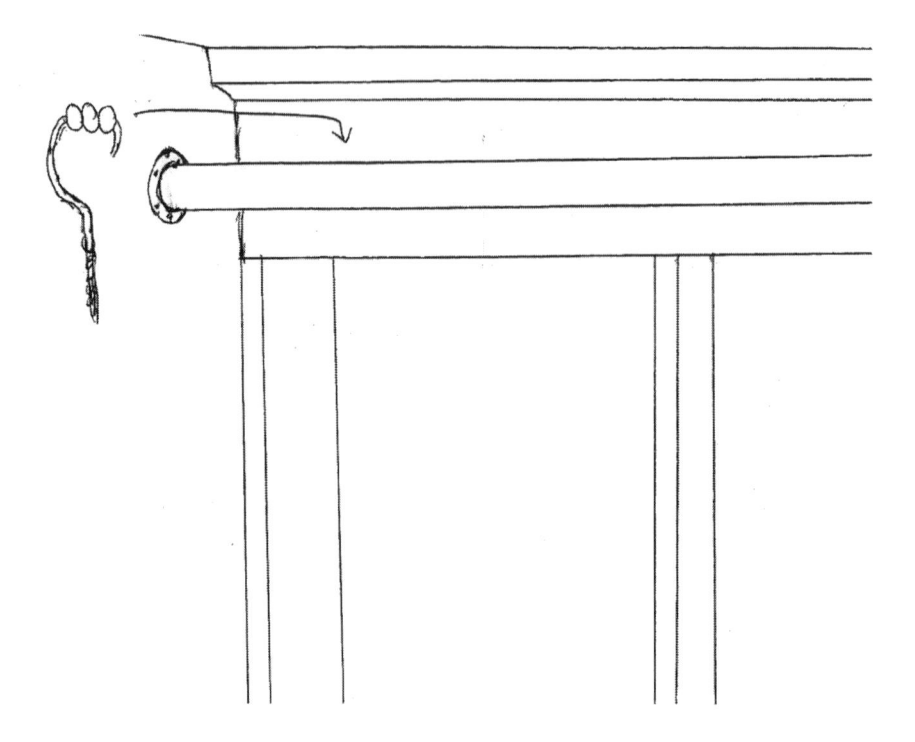

Notice that above in Figure Eleven, you can see the guide rail for the mobile stepper. When installing the rail, you want to make sure that the hooks will fit around the rail. Use some rounded beads with a hole large enough to fit onto the hook for easy rolling.

Figure Twelve: The bottom of the mobile stepper

Figure 12a   Figure 12b
   Figure 12c

Notice the three steps in making the mobile stepper. First, you want to build the two steps as shown in Figure 12a. Then, as shown in Figure 12b, you want to add some wheels on the bottom of the stepper so it can roll across the floor in front of the shelves. Then, Figure 12c illustrates the entire mobile stepper as it is placed on the track at the top of the shelves. You want to pay close attention to make sure the two 2X2s you are using to attach the stepper to the guide rail at the top are the exact measurement to ensure stability.

Decorative Wall Shelves
These are small shelves and do not take much effort to build. Basically, uses for a decorative wall shelf is to either store cookbooks in your kitchen or different trinkets, collectables, or souvenir items in other rooms.

Building a decorative wall shelf is quite simple. All you need to do is to find a couple of studs in the wall using a stud detector and mark them. Then you make the supports for the shelf as shown in Figure Thirteen below. After making the supports, you will want to drill pilot holes for the screws to screw each support into a stud. You can also use a back board to screw the supports to as shown in Figure Fourteen, what ever is easiest for you. Also, with the back board, you can make interesting edges to make it look decorative. You can also get wooden peg caps or putty at any home improvement store to cover the holes made by the screws.

Figure Thirteen: The decorative shelf supports

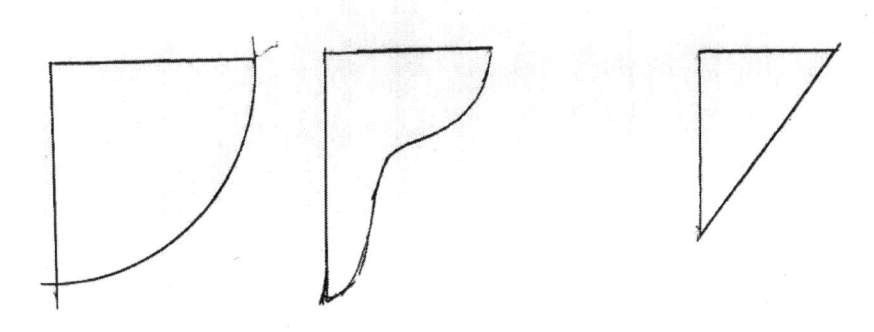

Notice in the image above, the support for the decorative shelf is the typical shape you see. You can make any shape you decide, from triangular to round, as long as the wood is deep enough to support the shelf and what will be on the shelf.

Figure Fourteen: The different ways to fasten the shelf supports to the wall

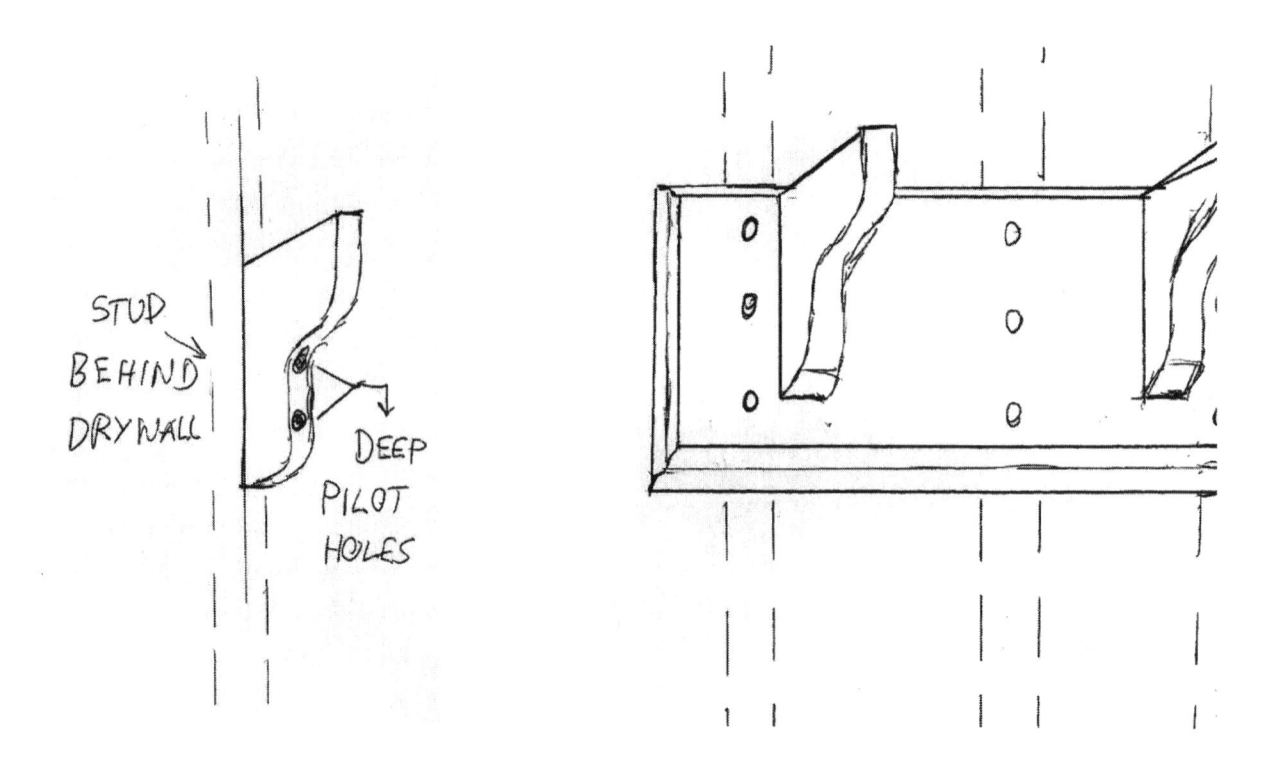

Figure 14a   Figure 14b

Notice that in Figure 14a, this is the most difficult method. You have to drill deep holes and have very long screws to fasten the support to the wall. The problem with this method is that you will have to make sure that the supports are also screwed into a stud.

Figure 14b, on the other hand, is much easier to do and more feasible for those of you who do not have any experience with good woodworking skills. It is much easier to screw the backboard to the stud than the simple support. Using a router with some special bits, you can also make a decorative rim on both the backboard and the shelf supports.

The shelf can be made in all kinds of shapes. You can also make the shelf match the support board as shown in Figure 14b.

Building Movable Shelf or Book Cases
Sometimes, you want furniture which has shelving in it. The typical type of such furniture is the bookcase or you can also build a combination of shelves and cabinets, for a stereo or TV set. We will cover a multifunctional piece of furniture with shelves and cabinets later. Here, however, we will focus on the more simple, such as a standard bookcase which you can move around when you rearrange a room or take with you when you move to another location.

Building a bookcase is similar to the methods we covered in the previous chapter about making kitchen cabinets, but without the cabinetry. You also do not need as much skeletal structure when building a bookcase. Building a bookcase is rather simple. The basic steps are explained below.

A. **Take three boards of fine wood** and screw them together with finish screws. If you want the shelves to be adjustable, then you will need to carve the grooves with a special bit from a router. You can also use your router to carve slots in which the shelves can slide in. Either way, that needs to be done before you screw the vertical shelf walls to the base shelf.
B. **Screw the back board** into place and then you will have the basic shelf box already almost done.
C. **Screw the top** onto the top of the vertical shelf walls and you already have the entire box complete.
D. **Insert the shelves into place** and move the bookcase where you want it to be.

That's basically there is to it. Use care in height or width. Check with your local lumber yard to see what size wood panels you have.

Shelves are needed for many things. Hopefully this chapter has given you the instructions on how to best build the kinds of shelves you need and the rest is up to you.

Chapter Four

Wardrobe Closets and Armoires

Storage can be an issue for many people. Many people who live in high efficiency apartments, condos, and small houses have very limited closet space or space to store shoes, clothes, and other items which we usually like to place in a closet.

In this chapter you will learn how to build ideal furniture for storage of shoes, clothes, kitchen goods, and hanging hooks for coat and hat racks. The items you will learn in this chapter will be listed below.

A. **Armoires** and what they are. What exactly is an armoire? Basically, an armoire is a French word which depicts a tall upright storage cabinet which is movable. Armoires can be built for your kitchen, garage, storage shed, or workshop. You can incorporate shelving in an armoire as well.
B. **Wardrobe closets** are basically a closet made for clothes and is not fixed into a permanent structure. Wardrobes also have small shelves in the bottom in which you can store shoes. You can also get a shoe rack which can be screwed to the inside of the doors and store your shoes that way.
C. **Shoe storage space bed combos** are a great idea for those of you who like to have a lot of shoes and have very limited space to store them all.
D. **Coat and hat racks** are ideal for your foyer and should include a bench for you to be able to sit down and tie or untie your shoes, put on or take off shoes, etc.

Armoires
Though armoires were more popular in from the 18th to the mid 20th Centuries than they are now, they can be a good thing to have. Armoires can be great for people who often move because of their jobs or are in the military. What ever the reason, an armoire can be used as a movable general storage cabinet. Uses for an armoire are as follows:

A. **Kitchen utensils** or added space for storing canned goods, paper plates, pots and pans, etc.
B. **Guns and fishing rods** along with ammunition. You can include everything for the great outdoors and store all the things you need for your hunting and fishing trips, including guns, knives, fishing rods, lures, or fishing tackle.
C. **Paints and brushes** for those of you who have an active hobby room. You can have an armoire to store art supplies, such as acrylic and oil paints, watercolors, brushes, palates, canvases, and more.
D. **General storage** of miscellaneous things that you don't need all the time. Seasonal items, such as Christmas, 4th of July, or other holiday decorations can be stored in a nice armoire which is out of the way and nicely kept when they are not up.

The basic construction of an armoire is rather easy to build. Building an armoire is basically like building a box with two front doors which open outward. The ideal hinges for armoire doors are piano hinges, as they are long and slender and out of the way.

There are many different locks which you can use to lock your armoire. If you are building an armoire to store your guns and knives, you should have a lock on it. This especially holds true if you have children. Even fishing tackle should be locked up, as the sharp fish hooks can be dangerous when around small children. Different locks are listed below.

A. **Padlocks** are by far the easiest locks to use when locking an armoire. You can simply lock your armoire with a padlock using a loop and latch on which the latch has a slot which the loop passes through the slot. The padlock is then placed into the loop and locked. You can also use a bolt which slides across both doors and the bolt has a loop which goes over a corresponding loop affixed to a fixed area above or beneath the bolt. The padlock goes through both loops and the bolt is locked into place.
B. **Mechanical lock** which requires a key can also be used. These locks work by having a bolt which slides behind the doors on the inside and moves by turning the key.
C. **Magnetic locks** are designed if you do not want to lock your armoire with a key. Magnetic locks are the same thing you have to keep your kitchen cabinets closed. Two magnets are placed to attract each other and the magnetic pull holds the doors shut.

Building the armoire should start with a plan. You should use one inch thick plywood or wooden planks. If you like to have your armoire in an area where you have friends over or where you entertain, then you can make it fancy with carving on the doors or doing other detail work on it.

When choosing the wood to build your armoire, you have a variety of different woods to choose from. Typical woods for fine furniture would be aspen, walnut, poplar, mahogany, or oak. If you have money to spend, you can even get more exotic woods, such as teak or ebony.

Build the base first by taking a couple of 2X6s and screw on the floor of the armoire. You can then add the two support walls and 2X2s for the corners. Be sure to cover the 2X6s and 2X2s with the fine wood and make everything flush with each other. Leave some space above at the top so you can add a crown board or crown molding for a fancier armoire.

You need the 2X2s for hinge posts. Simply screw the piano hinges on and hang the doors. That's basically the basics for a typical armoire construction for your home. See Figures One and two for basic armoire construction with minor skeletal construction.

Figure One: The standard armoire construction

As shown in Figure One, the basic construction of the armoire is a basic armoire, in which you can easily screw in some shelf supports and use this like a cupboard to store non-perishable foods, hobby items, or other bulk items which simply need to be out of the way, like seasonal items.

Figure Two: An armoire constructed to support racks or hanger bars.

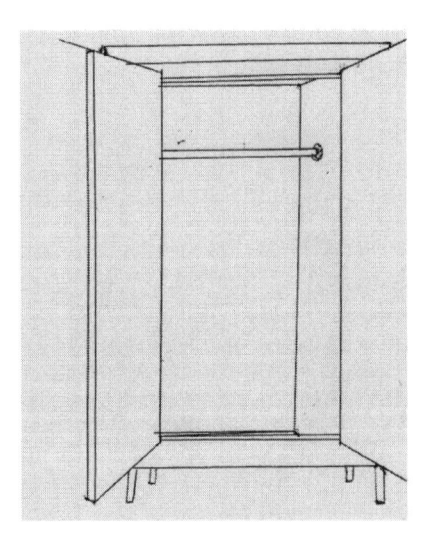

As you notice in Figure Two, you can use this construction to build a solid gun rack which can hold your long guns, fishing rods, and even have special racks for your pistols and handguns. The type of skeletal construction shown in Figure Two above can also be used to have a hanger bar so you can hang clothes on coat hangers in it. The hanger bar is great for storing your best clothes, pants, suites and keep them from getting wrinkled. The base support can also be used to make a storage space for shoes.

Building a gun rack is great if you are an avid hunter, fisherman, or love marksmanship. There are several ways you can build a gun rack.

The rack is ideal for rifles, shotguns, and a wide variety of fishing rods. You also have a storage space below where you can store your munitions canisters, fishing tackle, and reloading machines for your shotgun shells. We do recommend you have a strong lock on your armoire if you want to use it to store guns. If you have some handguns you want to store with your long guns, you can easily modify the rack or make special side racks to store the handguns.

Installing a hanger rod and shoe storage is very simple. To make the hanger rod, simply get a dowel rod which is about one inch in diameter. Get fastening hardware and screw it to the supports. You can also get metal hanger rods which telescope out to size and all you need to do with those is simply telescope it so it is as long as your armoire is wide and screw the ends to the different supports. Simply make a shelf with dividers in the bottom and you have a small space to store your shoes. If you have a lot of shoes to store, you can also buy pre-made shoe racks which are easy to assemble and simply screw onto the doors at any home improvement store.

Keeping your armoire doors locked and not able to be opened when locked with a key is also a very simple solution. On one door, from the inside simply screw on a bolt on the top and bottom of the door. Drill a hole in the 2X2 both on top and on the bottom. The bolts are a manual lock with a handle which you can twist and move up or down and twist to lock the door in place. Then simply use the lock of your choice on the door without the bolts. It's that simple. The doors will stay locked strongly and you won't have to worry whether anyone will be able to access the contents of your armoire who is not supposed to.

Building your Wardrobe Closet
Basically, building your wardrobe closet is pretty much the same as building an armoire. Simply follow the directions above and you have most of the techniques to make your wardrobe closet. The only difference is that wardrobe closets should be a bit bigger than an armoire so it can store more clothes. Use the hanger bar to hang all your shirts, coats, suits, dresses, and other article of clothing which requires a coat hanger.

Shoe storage in a wardrobe closet can be done in a variety of ways. You can have a pre-made shoe rack or a shelf for shoes at the bottom of the closet, but there are also different types of shoe storage devices which have a coat hanger hook on them which you can hang on the hanger rod. If you make a rather large wardrobe closet, there should be ample space for that.

Shoe Storage Bed Space Combos
Though building beds and headboards are covered in another chapter, this chapter is all about storage in tight living quarters. Because there are many of you who have kids who are college students and live in a dorm room or rent an apartment with other kids, you need some ideas for furniture and have the ability to store shoes, clothes, and other items. What a better idea than building a bed with a trundle drawer which instead of storing another mattress can store shoes.

This is very easy to build. Simply use some good wood to make a structure large enough for a bed for one person. Basically this is much like a bed on a large wooden box. The items you will need to work on this project are as follows:

A. **2X4s** for the skeletal structure of the storage box
B. **Fine wood in board form** to build the sides and storage drawers
C. **Plywood** to make dividers in drawers
D. **A basic mattress** without box springs

Construct the skeleton of the bed using the 2X4s. Typically, beds are about six feet long and four feet wide. You will want to get a mattress first and take measurements of it. See Figure Five below to see how the skeletal structure should look for the bed shoe storage combo. Note that the top should have more 2X4s for supports than the bottom or the sides. Likewise, you may want to build a wall in the middle of the storage unit to support the weight of a person lying down.

Since the top of the storage unit will be covered by a mattress, you do not need to have decorative expensive wood on that part. A good piece of fine plywood sanded down will do. You should incorporate railings with the wood on the top part of the storage unit which can hold the mattress in place.

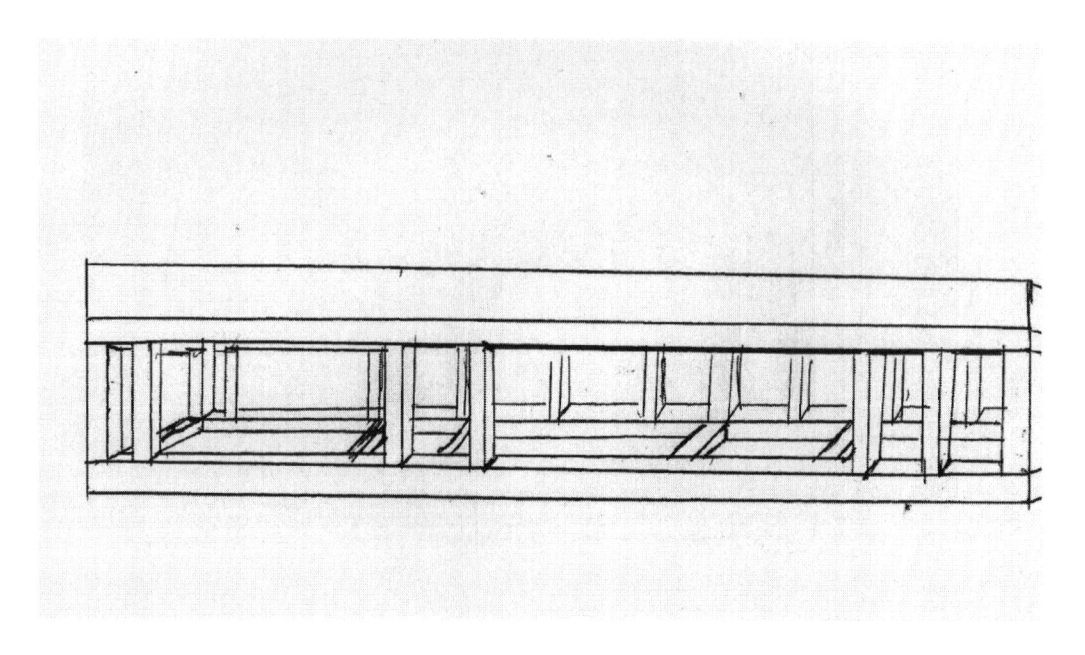

Figure Four: The skeletal structure of the bed and storage combo.

Notice that in Figure Five above, you have the most 2X4 support for the bed part of the unit. The reason is because that will bare the brunt of the weight of the person sleeping on the bed.

You do not want to build this bed too high. Just build it high enough do someone can simply climb into it without having to climb a ladder or step to get to bed.

Building the drawers can be done without sliders, though you can find some heavy duty sliders and there should be two drawers on either side, unless the bed is positioned next to a wall. The drawers should have dividers which can fit any size pair of shoes. This means that the compartments within the drawers should hold up to a pair of size 12, which is about a foot in length. See Figure Six below to see how the drawers and their compartments should be made.

Figure Five: The drawer with shoe compartments

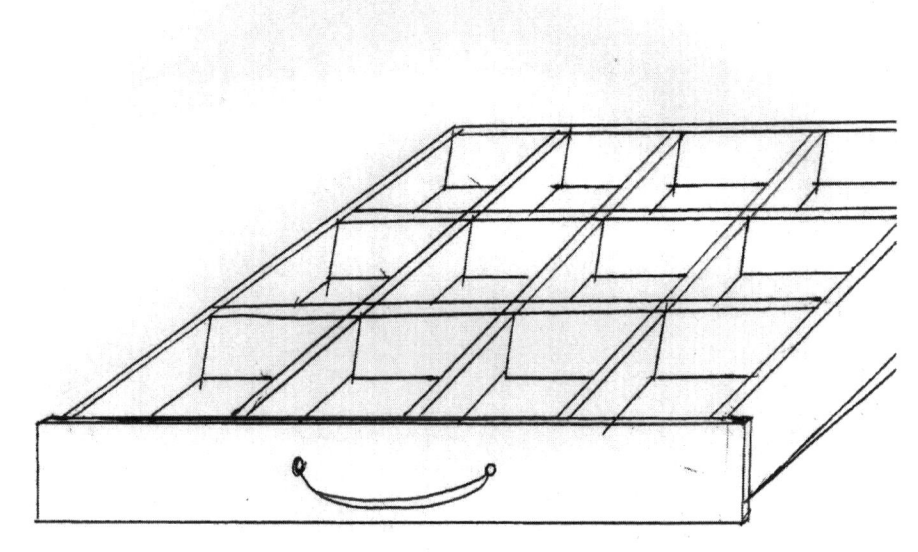

Completing the project is simply putting all the finished panels in place and add the mattress and bed sheets. You are ready to go. Also, don't forget a nice pillow for extra comfort. Now you have created a bed with plenty of shoe storage for your college bound child.

Coat and Hat Racks
Typically, when you think about a coat and hat rack, you tend to think about a round stand on which you can hang your hats and coats on. That's fine for a small business or place where people can take their hats and coats off when they will be at an office for a while, but at home, it's a completely different story.

The foyer, your coats, hats, and shoes can be a mess. You definitely need some organization in this part of the house, as it is the part which everyone sees and is the entrance of your home. This is also where everyone tracks mud and dirt into the house with their boots and shoes.

Building a hat and coat rack is rather easy. All you need is a heavy base and a light top. The key is not to have the rack be top heavy. The base can also be designed to have shoe compartments to store your shoes which you use for that season, so for example, in the winter time, boots, in the spring and fall, sneakers and warm shoes, in the summer sandals and flip-flops. You can also store your dress shoes for your Sunday best. You can use the bench to sit on as you are putting your shoes on and off. If you wear shoes or slippers inside, then you should also have a place to put them so they don't get dirty from your outside shoes.

Building the bench is fairly easy. Simply build a regular box, but have the shoe compartment easy to get to. There are two ways you can build the bench, one with the shoes visible and the other with the shoes inside the bench with a hinged top. See Figure Six below on how both benches look.

Figure Six: Bench style

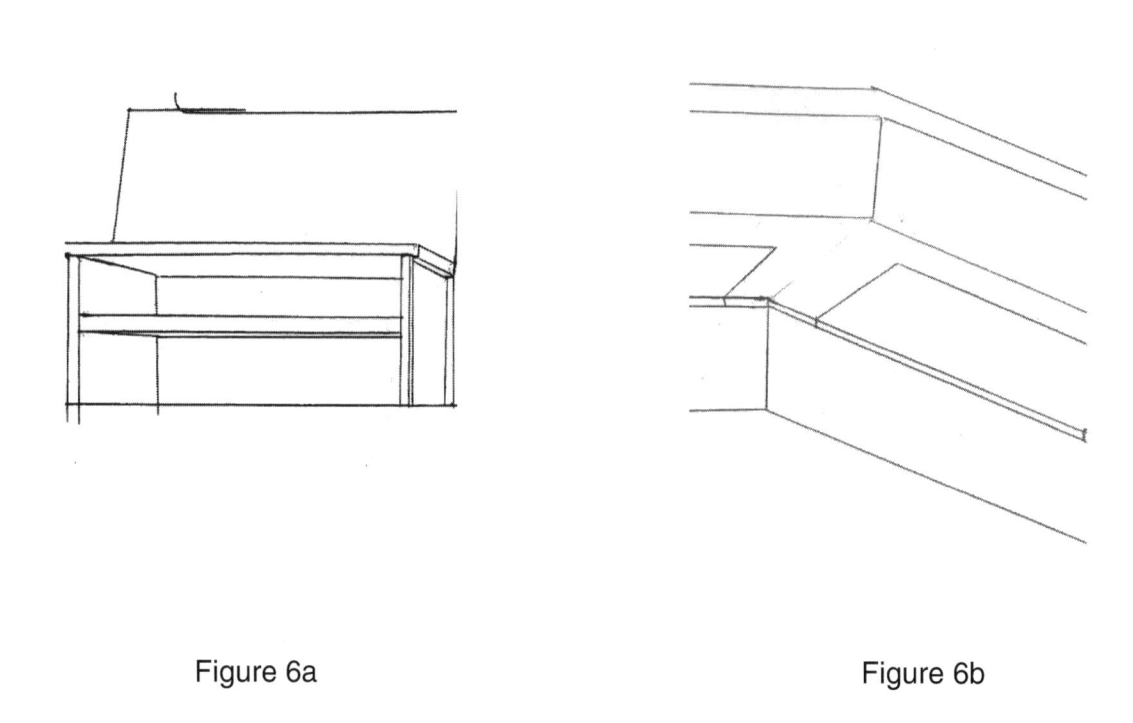

Figure 6a   Figure 6b

Building the back which holds the rack is very simple also. All what the back does is support the coat and hat racks. Some even have a small shelf for both hats, gloves, and mittens.

When building the back, use a couple of 2X8s on either side parallel to the sides of the bench. Then you can simply use a couple of 2X4s on which you can add a cross board with the hooks to hang your coats on. See Figure Eight below for the finished product.

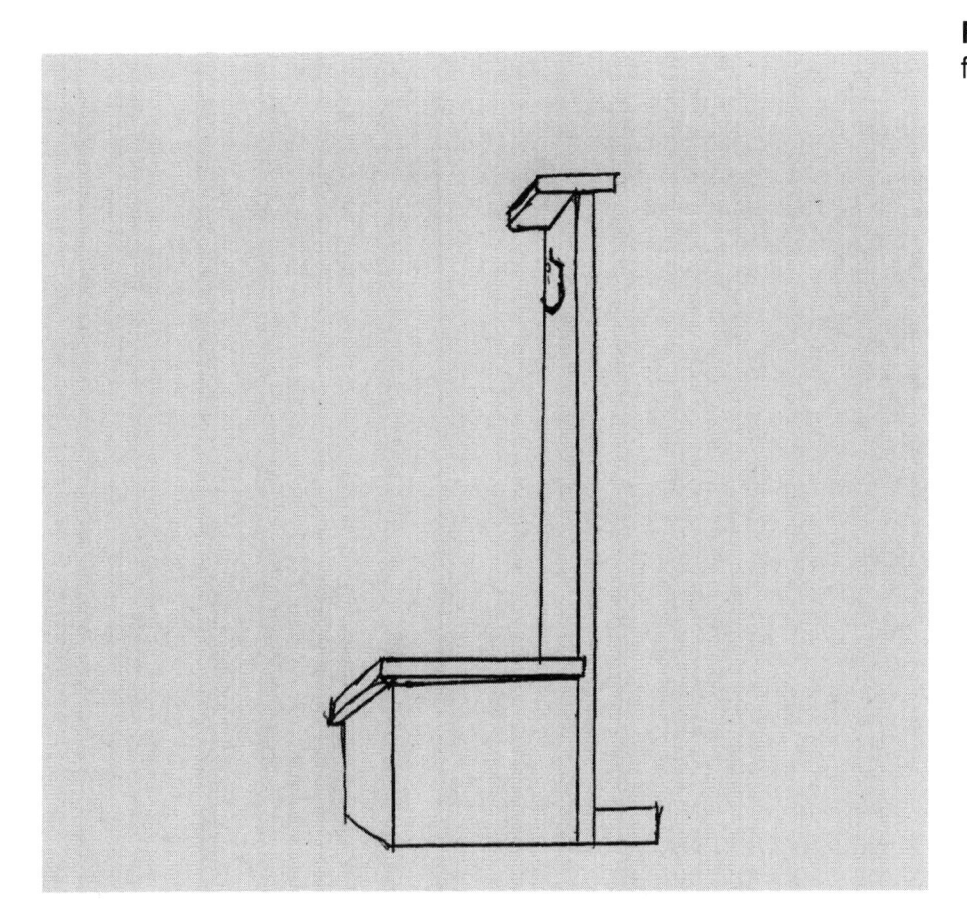

Figure Seven: The finished product.

Ideal for your foyer and easy to build, this is a necessary piece of furniture. A home looks so much better when your coats are hanging neatly on a coat rack and your shoes are hidden away and not seen as much. This will look so much better than coats strewn across your couch or a chair.

Storage units are very important for every household. From big mansions to the small hole-in-the-wall apartments, having the right storage space can sometimes be critical. Using armoires, wardrobe closets, shoe storage under beds, and hat and coat racks are sometimes the right options.

Chapter Five

Dressers, Desks, and Other Furniture with Drawers

One of the most difficult things to build is something which has drawers. There all kinds of storage fixtures and furniture which contain drawers. These can range from kitchen cabinets to bathroom vanities for fixed items to desks, dressers, and night stands which all have drawers in them. Here you will learn how to do the following projects.

- **A. Methods of drawer making:** Learn how to make the basic drawer. You will learn how to make any type of drawer and have the skills for the projects listed below. Learn how to dove tail and other corner construction for drawers.
- **B. A closer look in making and repairing drawers** for your kitchen cabinets or bathroom vanity. You will learn how to have different sliders for drawers, such as track rollers for your kitchen cabinets and grooved sliders for most bathroom vanities.
- **C. Building different types of desks:** Learn how to build desks from the simple to the elegant. Learn about doing desk drawers, different options for desk top, making a slider for your laptop or computer keyboard.
- **D. Build a dresser** for your bedroom. Learn how to properly make drawers which hold all your undergarments, socks, seasonal clothing, jewelry, and more. Learn the different style of drawers you can make for your dresser.
- **E. Build a night stand** to have next you your bed. Most night stands have one drawer and a cabinet or set of shelves beneath the drawer. Add accents and functionality to your night stand, such as electrical outlets for an alarm clock, night lamp, or charger for your cellphone.

Methods of Drawer Making
One of the most difficult and complicated aspects of woodworking is making drawers, however, we all need them and we all have cabinets where drawers are needed. Before you can build a cabinet or piece of furniture which requires drawers, you will need to learn how to make them.

There are several different ways to make a good sturdy drawer which can hold for a long time and will stay together.

Dove tailing is one of the most common and time tested method of making drawers which last. If you notice at older drawers from older pieces of furniture from the 19th Century and the early to mid 20th Century, you will notice a kind of squaring pattern on the backs of the drawers. This is dove tailing.

Dove tailing is called what it is because the tongues which are carved onto the edges of the wood which makes the drawer are shaped much like a dove's tail. You can see below how to make dove tails for your drawers in Figure One.

Figure One: The step by step process of dove tailing

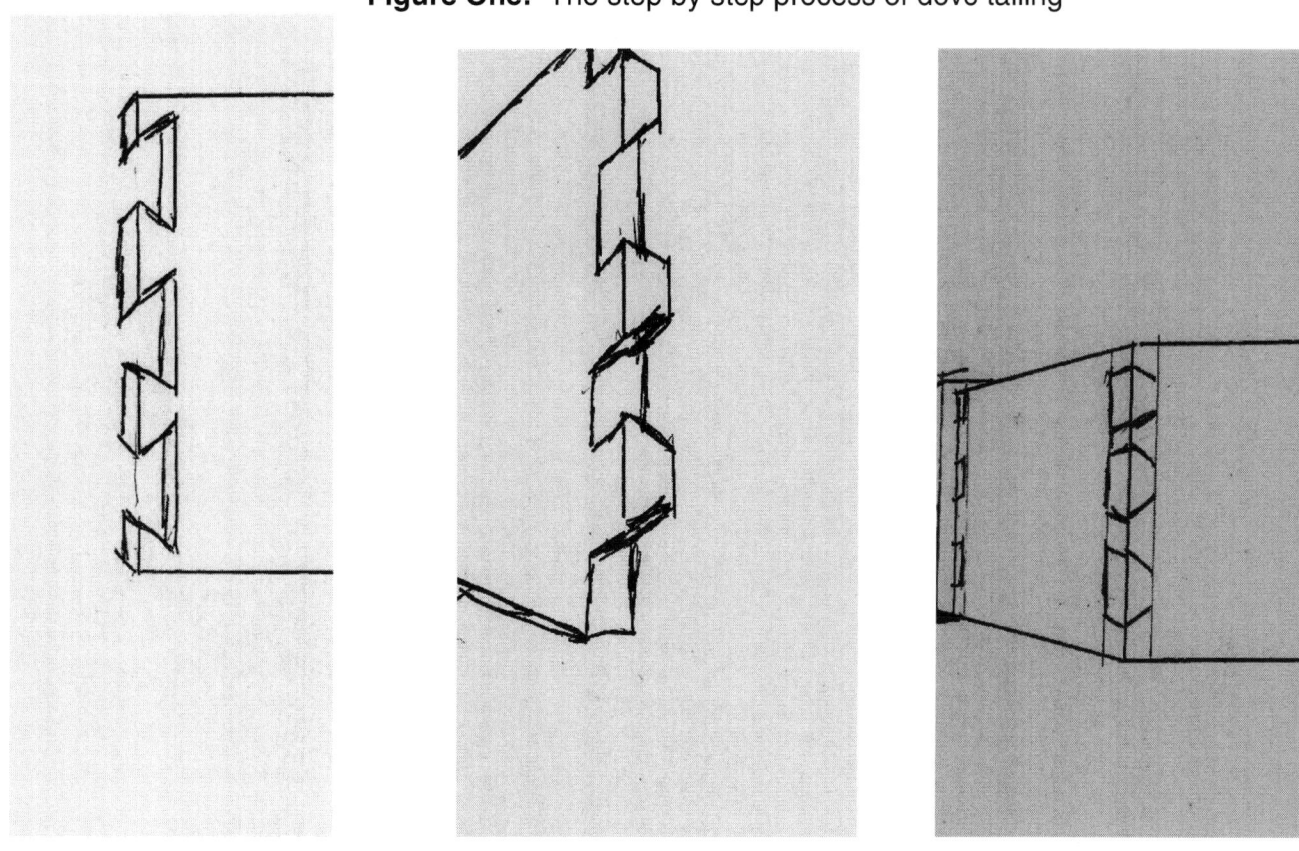

Figure 1a   Figure 1b   Figure 1c

Notice that in Figure 1a, the back board is cut first. These tongues are cut in the shape of a dove's tail. Figure 1b shows the sides of the drawer carved in the shape of a dove's tail and Figure 1c shows how they interlock together.

What is great about the dove tailing method is that nails are not required. The dove tails themselves interlock and with a little bit of adhesive, you have a strong bond which will not go anywhere.

Dove tailing also looks very beautiful and many furniture makers today consider dove tailed drawers to be a sign of high quality workmanship.

Screws and braces can also be used in making drawers. Though this method is not as strong as the dove tails are, it is much simpler to do. Simply get for L-braces with corresponding screws from your local home improvement store, Menard's, Lowe's or Home Depot and you can simply fasten the drawer parts together.

Tongue and groove is another method which is commonly used when making drawers. With the tongue and groove method, you can get a special bit for your router to carve out a groove in the side boards of the drawer and a tongue in the back board. See Figure Two below.

Figure Two: Tongue and groove method for drawer construction

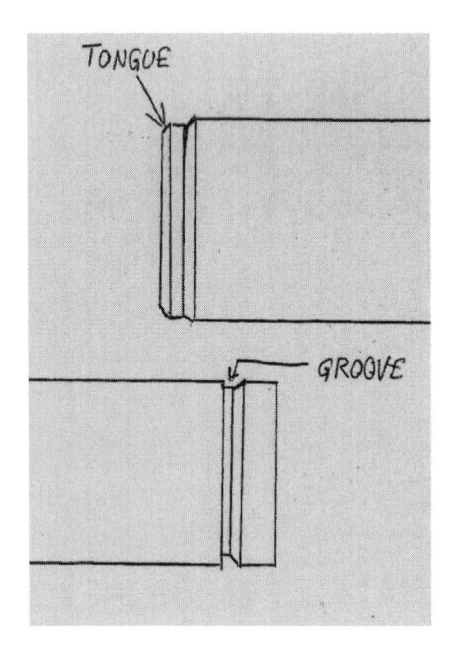

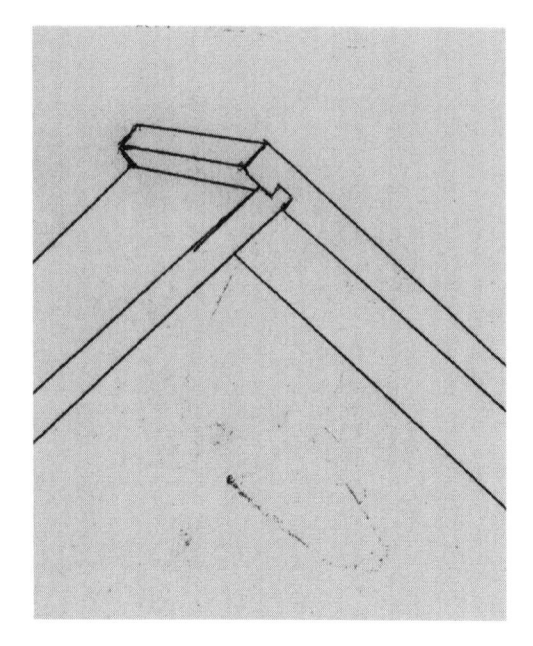

Figure 2a   Figure 2b

Notice with the same groove bit, you can also carve out a tongue with your router, which will fit into the groove of the side boards. Figure 2a illustrates the groove in the side board and the corresponding tongue in the back board. Figure 2b shows how the tongue and the groove fit together. We recommend that you use adhesive and finish nails to add some strength to reinforce the hold.

Sliders are just as important as the drawer construction itself. A slider facilitates the opening and closing of a drawer. You don't necessarily need to make a slider for your drawers. In fact, some older desks and dressers did not have sliders, but the sliders facilitate the drawer to open and close without much effort.

Roller sliders are a track which is fixed to the drawer shaft. Then on the drawer, a roller is attached. At the end of the track at the opening of the drawer shaft, there is a slight lump. This allows you to remove the drawer from the shaft if you have to. Simply slightly lift up the front of the drawer and place the rollers onto the track and it will then slide. The lump in the track will keep the drawer from sliding off the track and falling to the floor.

Groove sliders are another way you can arrange the drawer to easily slide open and closed. Basically, you can get a plastic groove which is affixed to the shaft and a tongue made from plastic affixed to the side of the drawer. Simply place the tongue into the groove and the drawer will slide in and out.

It's been our experience that using the roller slider track is the easiest to install and you can find roller sliders at any hardware or home improvement store.

A Closer Look at Making and Repairing Drawers
A big problem many people who have bought an old lived-in house is drawers in the kitchen cabinet or bathroom vanity which tends to jam or not open or close properly. Ideally, a kitchen drawer should easily slide open and closed. There are a variety of reasons why drawers jam and how you can fix them.

A. **A bent slider track** is the biggest culprit in drawers not sliding open and closed properly. Roller sliders have been around since the 1970s or even before. They have facilitated opening and closing drawers, but the one problem with older roller sliders is that they have a tendency of bending and that can cause the roller to derail and not move smoothly along the track. This can cause the drawer to get jammed in the shaft.
B. **Storing items higher than the shaft** is the second largest cause for drawers to jam and can also cause the drawer to derail its track and jamming being exacerbated creating a situation similar to problem A.
C. **Warped wood** can be a huge problem, especially in older houses which still have most of their original fixtures. Back in the days many older farmhouses and Victorian houses were built in the mid to late 19th century do not have sliders in their drawers. Some kitchen drawers may have a groove and tongue which were carved from wood, but because the wood has warped and expanded and contracted many times, these drawers can be very tightly set in their shafts as they have not been used for a long time. The solution for warped wood is simply to build whole new cabinets and install new sliders for easy opening and closing.

Broken or loose front panels or parts of the back of the drawer breaking off can sometimes be a problem. Typically, this is not a major problem in older houses, like Victorians, as in those days most drawers were dove tailed, thus they are fairly durable. Houses built in the late 1970s to the mid 1980s, however, this can be a serious problem. The reason for this happening is that in the 1970s many cabinets and drawers were made from particle board instead of real wood.

Particle board was the novelty of the day in the 1970s. In fact, it has been around since the mid 1960s, but people did not realized that particle board at the time was about as flimsy as sheetrock or drywall. There are different types of particle board today, some of which use broad wooden chips which are put together with a powerful heat cured adhesive and is primarily used as floor paneling and wall covering in construction. In the 1960s and 1970s, particle board was made from fine wood particulates which could easily unravel and fall apart if it got wet. Particle board is not strong enough to hold wood screws and nails like real wood. These drawers cannot be fixed or salvaged. You may like the dated look of the 1970s or 1980s for several sentimental reasons. This was probably the time of your childhood. Possibly you may have gotten married in that era. That's fine, but you can always recreate that look with new cabinets, especially if you build them from scratch, as you are being taught in this book. You want to use real wood to build drawers and stay away from particle board.

Building Different Types of Desks
Everyone needs a desk of some sort. You also have different tastes and needs, thus your desk should be your own. Desks have evolved over time and now they have completely different functions with the advent of technology.

What exactly is a desk? Basically, a desk is a special table which has a combination of a table and a set of drawers. In the past, a desk was used as a writing table, drawing or drafting, running spreadsheets, and the like. Today, however, we do all of this on a computer. Rarely do you see someone take out a piece of paper and a fountain pen to write a paper or letter anymore. Now you have a computer with a word processor to write everything. Penmanship is not even an issue anymore because of new technology.

Like desks, computers have changed also. Back in the late 1990s when the first Apple MacIntosh and the first IBM PC came out, you had a bulky computer tower with a large monitor with a keyboard. Sometimes you needed a separate computer desk to accommodate those archaic computers so you could have a space for writing checks or other things.

Today, on the other hand, desk top computers are compact with a flat monitor which doesn't take up half the desktop, the keyboard can be tucked on a special flat drawer which can be closed when the computer is not in use. Desktop computers are also not as used as often as laptops and tablets. This gives you even more space on your desk. Now, the question is how can you build the right desk for your home office?

The basic desk for today's needs is fairly simple to build. The ideal desk needs to be designed to accommodate both a laptop or a desktop computer. This means you will need to make the following:

A. **One or two columns with drawers** to hold a wide variety of office supplies. These drawers should be big enough to hold pens, staplers and staples, check books and boxes of checks, printer paper, and other things you need.
B. **A keyboard drawer** is needed, especially if you have a desktop computer.
C. **A monitor shelf** to support a monitor for those who have a desktop computer
D. **A lower printer table** if you have a wired printer. If you have a wifi printer, you can literally have it in any part of the office.

The basic construction of a desk which meets today's needs is rather simple. Basically, you want to have some of the basic construction as you would in the traditional desk. Build the columns on both sides which can have three to four drawer shafts each. One column should have a filing drawer so you can store files of hard copies or files of bills, receipts, tax returns, or other important documents. In the middle, you should have a special shaft for a keyboard drawer. See Figure Three below to get the idea of how the basic desk construction should look like. This is before you install any of the drawers.

Figure Three:
The basic construction of a 21st Century desk

Notice that you have two columns for your drawers on both sides. The middle between the two drawer columns should be a space large enough to fit a desk chair or a space large enough to comfortable stretch your legs while working.

Notice in the middle of the desk beneath the desktop are two separate 1X2s on either side. This is where the roller slider for the keyboard drawer are to be installed.

Installing the drawers can simply be done by following the directions for making the drawers. You will have to measure space for the drawers if you plan to install roller sliders for the drawers.

Making the keyboard drawer is simply done by taking a wood panel which is about a half inch thick and attach a roller slider to allow the keyboard drawer to move in and out as you access your keyboard for a desktop. The keyboard drawer can also be a great place to store your laptop and have the charger cable for your laptop available.

Electrical fittings can be incorporated for your desk. Though electrical fixtures, such as electrical outlets were never installed into desks in the past simply because there was no need for them back them. Ideally, you want to install wall outlets in an area where they are not visible. This can easily be done. If you have an electrical outlet nearby, you want to get a powerful surge protector and have wall outlets installed under the monitor shelf. You can then have a wire with a male plug in the back of the desk to easily plug into a surge protector or wall outlet. Find someone who knows how to wire a plug to avoid a fire.

Building a Dresser
Dressers or commodes are a large set of drawers which you have in your bedroom to store small articles of clothing, such as undergarments, socks, pajamas, T-shirts, etc. Dressers can come in all kinds of different shapes and sizes. Some of them can even be equipped with a mirror for shaving and putting on makeup.

Building a dresser with a mirror panel may seem complicated, but it is fairly easy. This can actually pass for two projects in one. If you want to build a simple dresser to store clothing and don't care for the mirror, simply follow the basic instructions for the dresser.

Building the basic commode is the first step. You want to add special braces to hold the mirror panel which you can remove if you are planning to move. See Figure Four below to learn how the basic structure of the commode part of your dresser will look.

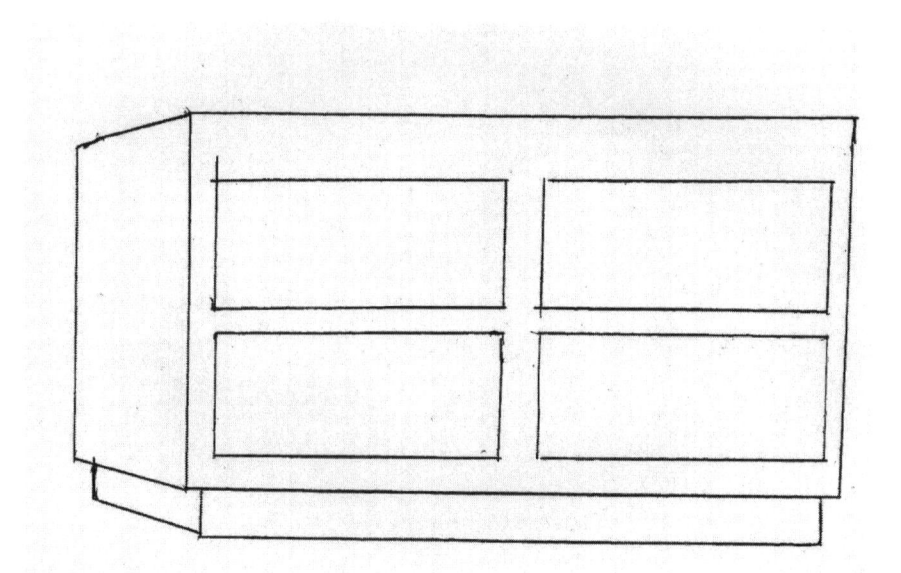

Figure Four: The basic commode section of your dresser.

If you notice above, this is the basic commode, which has a series of six large drawers. If you don't want to add the mirror, then you will not need to build the braces to support the mirror panel.

Note that the drawers in the commode need to be fairly large as they are designed to hold clothing. Your typical dresser should have six to eight drawers, depending on height. Ours has six drawers as the top can double as a make up table and you can also add smaller drawers and cabinets for jewelry, cosmetics, nail polish, perfumes, and after shaves.

Adding the mirror is complicated and you need to have very strong braces to support a large mirror. Mirrors are heavy as the mirror glass can be thick and is heavy by itself. When you add

it to a wood frame, then it is even heavier. Furthermore, the mirror needs to be removable incase you need to move the dresser from room to room or incase you move to a different dwelling.
When building the entire mirror structure, you also need to take into account ceiling height. Dressers can be very cumbersome pieces of furniture to move, and the average ceiling height in most middle to low income houses is anywhere from eight to ten feet from the floor. Likewise, the average doorway is seven feet high and three feet wide. Your entire dresser unit should be large enough to hold all your basic clothing which does not hang, but should be wide enough to fit through the average doorway.

Figure Five below shows the best way to create the supports for the mirror. You need to have a very heavy bottom to support the weight of the mirror. Basically, you want to take three short pieces of 2X8s and screw them together or you can also use metal brackets you can find at any hardware store. You simply use 2X8s and have nuts and bolts which can be used to secure the mirror panel to the commode.

Getting the glass for the mirror can be a big challenge. Mirror glass is different from ordinary glass. In many cases, mirror glass has to be special ordered. You typically cannot get mirror glass at your local Menard's, Lowe's, or Home Depot. They typically only sell mirrors which are a part of a medicine cabinet for your bathroom, which is already one unit. To get mirror glass, you will have to go to a special glass wholesaler who custom cuts glass pains. Even many of these glass wholesalers do not carry mirror glass, as there is not a high enough demand for it. Thus, they may have to special order it for you. Furthermore, the glass has to be delivered by a special delivery truck which has special racks to carry glass without breaking it.

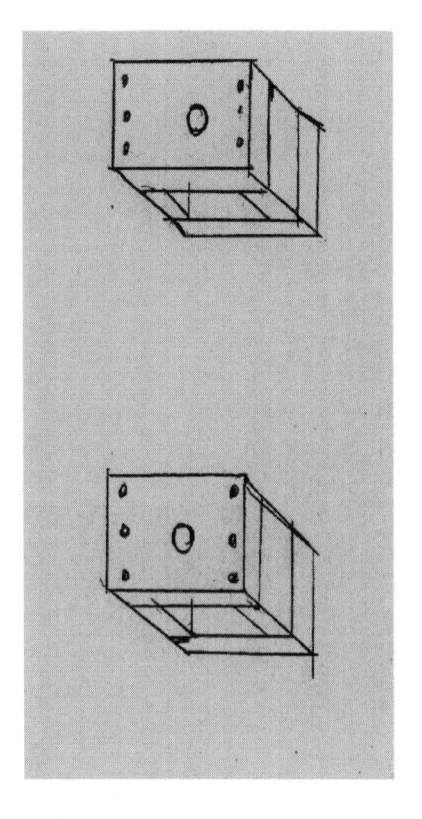

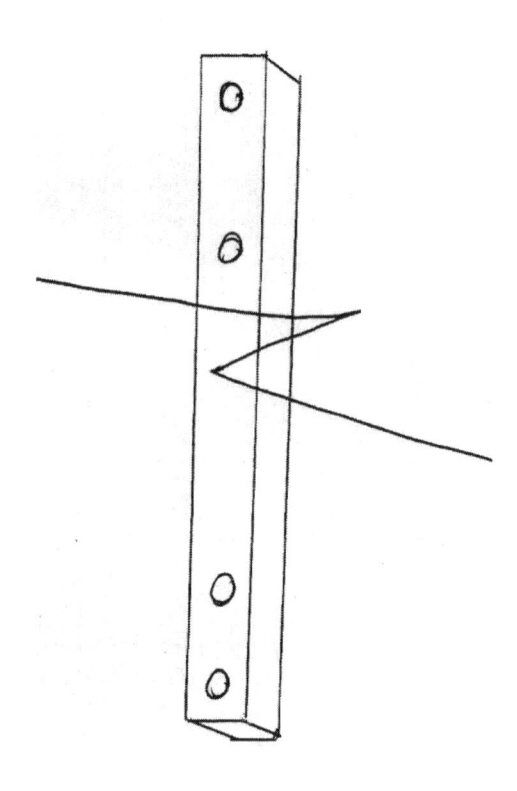

Figure Five: Wooden holders and metal brackets to hold the supports of the mirror panel
Figure 5a   Figure 5b

Notice that the wood braces can be fairly strong, but when it comes to weight, they can be fairly heavy. You can get special braces which are typically designed for decks and these are usually made from galvanized steel.

Building the mirror panel is challenging. You have a variety of options of style. If you want a Victorian look, you can have a glass merchandiser cut you an oval panel of mirror glass with a bevel and then you need to get a special large piece of fine wood on which you can fasten the mirror.

If you want the more modern look, then you can order the mirror glass in a square or rectangle. This is probably easier for you to construct if you are just a beginner in woodworking. Either way, you need special glass fasteners to affix the mirror glass to the wood panel. Look at Figure Six below on how to do this.

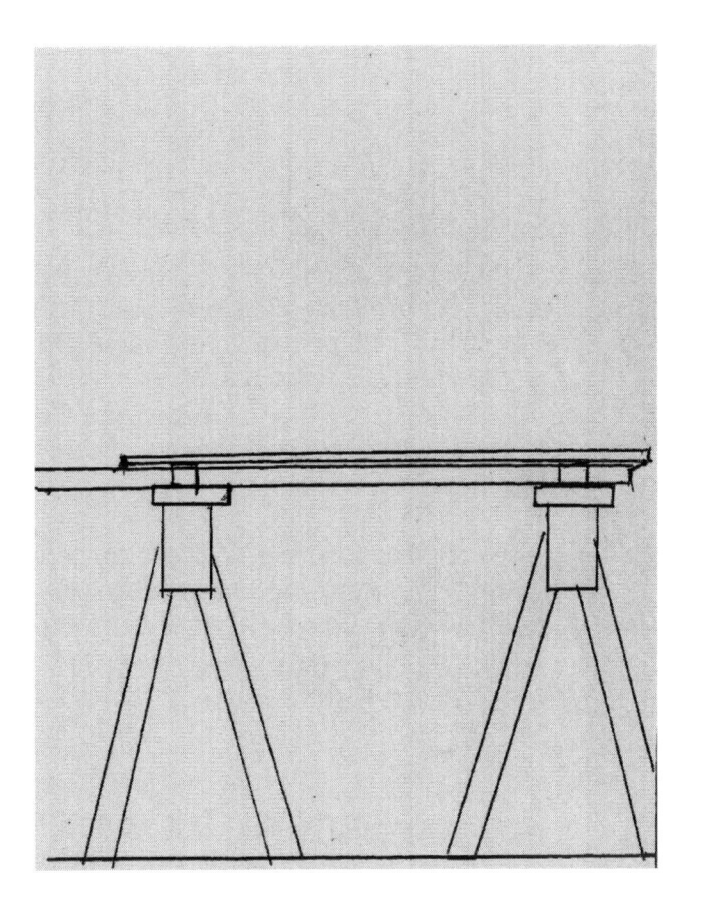

Figure Six: Affixing the mirror glass to the back wood panel

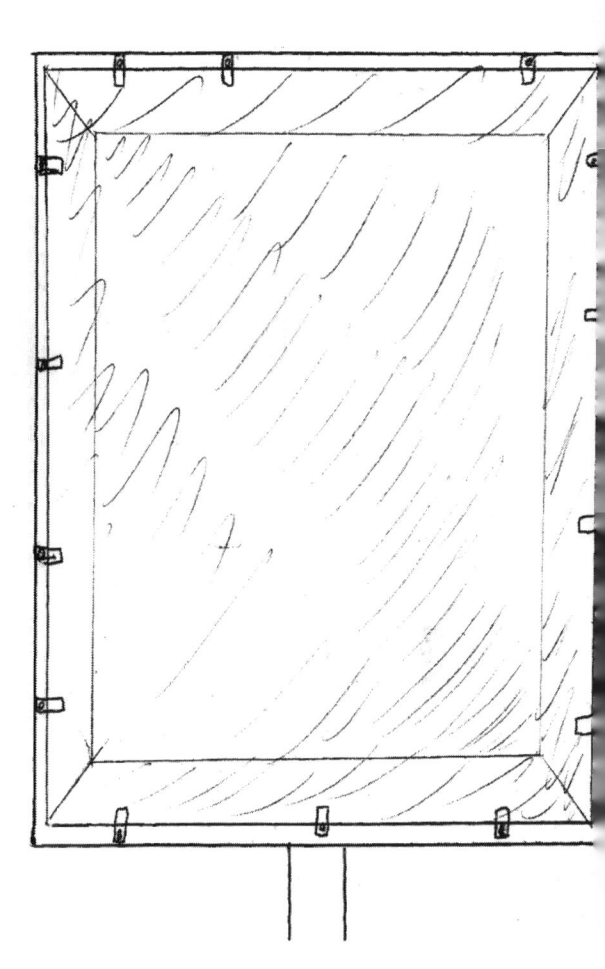

Figure 6a   Figure 6b

Notice in Figure 6a the wood panel is ready and is on a table horizontally. We recommend that you have the mirror horizontal when you install the glass. This eliminates the event of dropping the glass and shattering it. Care should be used in fastening it. You should lightly hammer the nails or screw in the fasteners by hand. Too much vibration can crack the glass.

Figure 6b shows how the mirror in the finished product. Notice that the 2X8s are not visible when the mirror panel is upright and affixed to the back of the commode.

Installing the drawers is done much like any other drawer. What you need to pay attention to, however, is that you need to have heavy duty roller sliders for your dresser drawers. Large drawers, such as dresser drawers or filing drawers can be heavy as they are made from wood and hold clothing, which is rather heavy.

Building a Night Stand
Building a night stand for your bedside is probably one of the easiest projects in this chapter. Basically, a night stand is a small table with a drawer directly underneath the top for items you will need during the night, such as medicine you need to take before bed time, a book you like to read before falling asleep, etc. The top of the night stand is just big enough to hold a lamp, a small speaker or set of mini-speakers for your iPod or MP3 player, if you like to listen to music when going to bed. Beneath the drawer you can have either a set of shelves or a cabinet for miscellaneous items.

Building the basic structure of the night stand is rather simple. All you need to do is find some 2X2s to build the skeletal structure and have something to screw the roller sliders into the drawer shaft. Then take some nice furniture quality wood panels to cover the skeletal structure. See Figure Seven below to get a good idea of how the basic night stand construction should look like.

Figure Seven: Basic night stand construction

Adding electrical power can also benefit your night stand, especially if you like high tech gadgets. Some mini speakers these days are a single unit and have a charging cradle on which the speaker unit can rest. Typically, the power source has rather short wires, thus you could benefit by installing a plug for those things.

Making the drawer and installing it is much like the rest of the projects, as is making the cabinet. Thus, you have a night stand which looks good and can also have some more storage space for other different items.

Learning how to make and install drawers is critical if you want to make furniture or do remodeling in your home.

Chapter Six

Tables and Chairs

Table and chair making is the epitome of building furniture. More important than drawer making, tables and chairs are the staple of a wide variety of furniture you need for your home. Whether you want to make a dining room set for formal dinners and get-togethers to the casual outdoor picnic or from the kiddy table and chairs to the andirondak chairs on your deck, the necessity for building your table and chairs is very necessary. In this chapter, you will learn all about tables and chairs and learn how to do the following projects.

- **A. Building your standard dining room set:** Learn how to build a dining room set with tables which even have fold out leaves for extra company and how to make the corresponding chairs.
- **B. Hard seats and upholstered seats:** Learn how to build a chair which can have a hard seat or do some minor upholstery.
- **C. Building a standard kitchen table with chairs:** Learn how to build a nice country style kitchen table which is circular in shape and folding leaves which can be down when only you are home and up when you have guests.
- **D. Building bar stools** for your bar in the basement or bar/countertop in your kitchen dinette area
- **E. Andirondak chairs** for your deck overlooking views of a lake or mountains. Learn how to build both the Andirondak chair and foot stool.
- **F. A front porch swing** which you can enjoy with your significant other on those warm summer evenings.

Building your Standard Dining Room Set

The dining room has always been that special room where you do not have your everyday meals. Typically, the purpose of the dining room is to entertain guests and have formal meals, either lunch or dinner. For this reason, your dining room set should be special. It should be the nicest table and chairs in the entire house.

Building the table is the first part of this project. A dining room table is more complicated than an ordinary table as it does have a leaf or two leaves to adjust the size to accommodate a large crowd. Ideally, when building a whole dining room set, you need to have a couple of extra chairs which match incase you have a lot of people coming.

The first step in building your dining room table is making the legs and then the top. You want the legs to be removable incase you need to move the table to another room, so the best way to make the legs is to get four 4X4s, one for each leg and cut them to be about four feet high. If you want the legs to look fancy, then you can use a lave to make the 4X4s round and carve beads which make for an interesting shape and design. See Figure One below how to operate a lave and carve the legs of the table. One thing you need to remember, however, is that you should leave the top of the legs square so you can have a fastening mechanism to bolt the legs securely to the table in a way the whole table won't collapse.

Figure One: Use of the lave and the finished product.

Figure 1a   Figure 1b

Notice in Figure 1a, the lave is used to carve beads into the wood and taper the foot part of the leg. As you notice in Figure 1a, the top part of the leg remains square. There is a reason for this. You will have to have a way of fastening the leg to the table. On the other hand, in Figure 1b, the table leg is finished with the lave, thus it's time to drill some bolt holes to drive a large bolt with a wing-nut to secure it to the table.

The table top does require some engineering to build, especially if you want the table to pull out and have an extension or a couple of extension leaves to extend your table for company.

The table top needs to be set on a movable skeleton, which should slide on a heavy duty roller slider. There are specialty shops which sell the special sliders for tables. We do advise looking online for the hardware needed for an extendable table, as this kind of hardware is not found in most hardware or home improvement stores. Even the major home improvement mass merchandisers, such as Menard's, Lowe's, or Home Depot probably don't carry this kind of hardware.

Constructing the table top begins with building a simple skeletal structure from 2X4s which go half the length of the table and have the skeleton should be reinforced on the corners and have a square large enough to fit a 4X4, which is what the legs originally were. You may want to fit the leg in the corner, then drill a bolt hole to make sure that the holes in the skeletal structure of the table top and the leg to insure the bolt goes through far enough to where you can tighten it snugly with a wing-nut.

Add a couple of 2X4s in the center with some fasteners to which you can affix the extension hardware. Take a look at Figure Two below to see how you need to build the skeletal structure with the extension sliders.

Figure Two: The skeletal structure of the dining room table top with the extension sliders

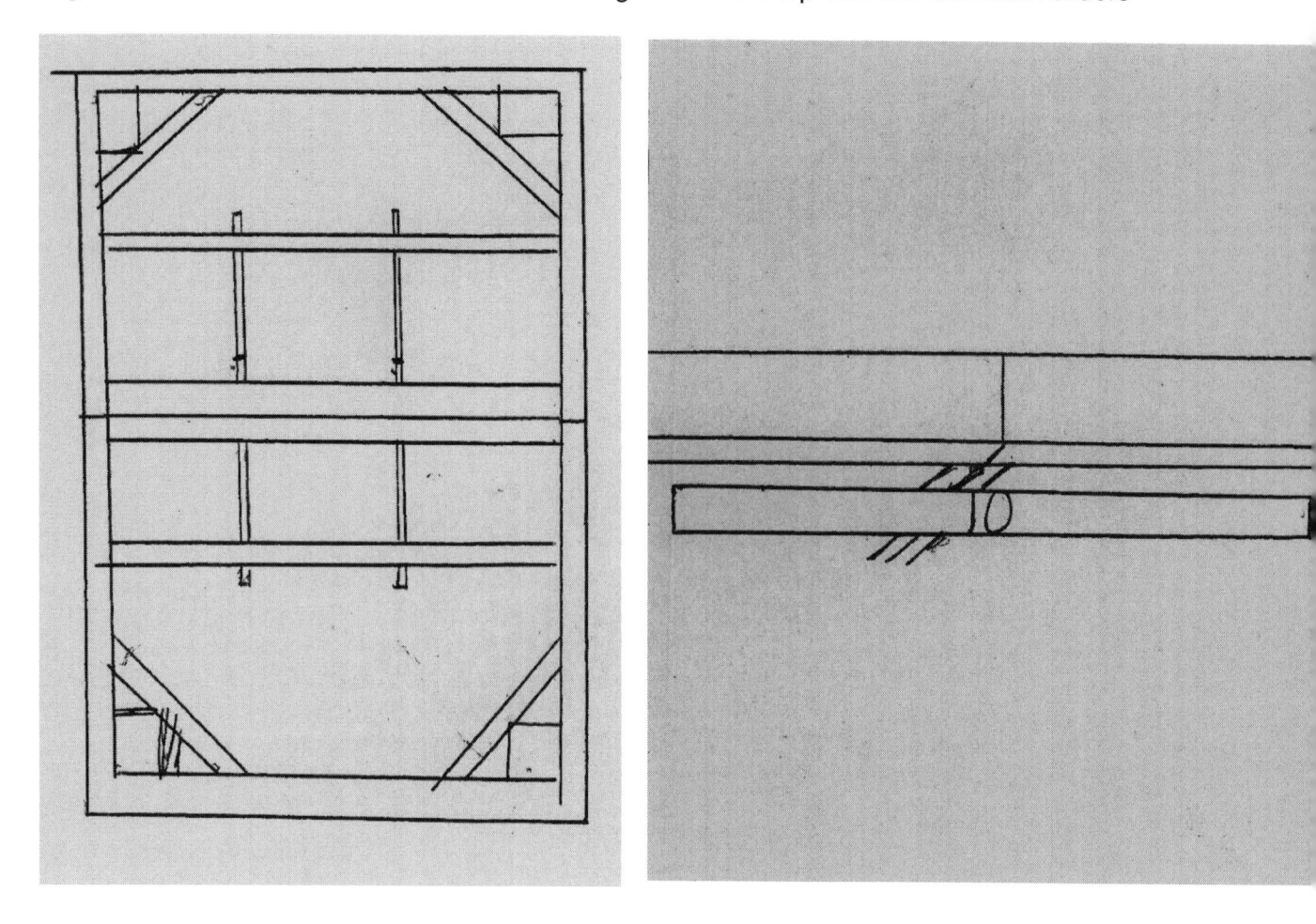

Figure 2a   Figure 2b

Choosing the wood for the table top should be left up to your personal tastes. Some of the finest woods around include aspen, maple, oak, pine, mahogany, walnut, or ebony. We do recommend you use the same wood for the legs as for the table top so everything matches. Looking for actual 4X4s of the finest woods requires some searching. You cannot find 4X4s at any lumberyard, so you will have to do some research and find a merchant who deals in fine woods and who's clientele are furniture makers. These merchants are more likely to have good quality woods.

Do note, if you are planning to work with a lave, do practice with regular wood first so you don't waste the fine expensive wood first.

Attaching the legs to the table can be a bit tricky. The easiest way to do that is to place the table top upside down and place the legs into their sockets and both them in. One caveat about fashioning the legs, however, keep the bottoms without patterns. This way you can temporarily place them in the table sockets and check with a water level to see if the top is level. If the table top is not level, you want to shave off thin slices of the longer legs until the table is level, which is indicated when the water bubble is exactly between the two lines marked on the glass tube of the level.

See Figure Three below to see how you should have the bolts installed and the legs properly fastened and have a sturdy table which won't collapse.

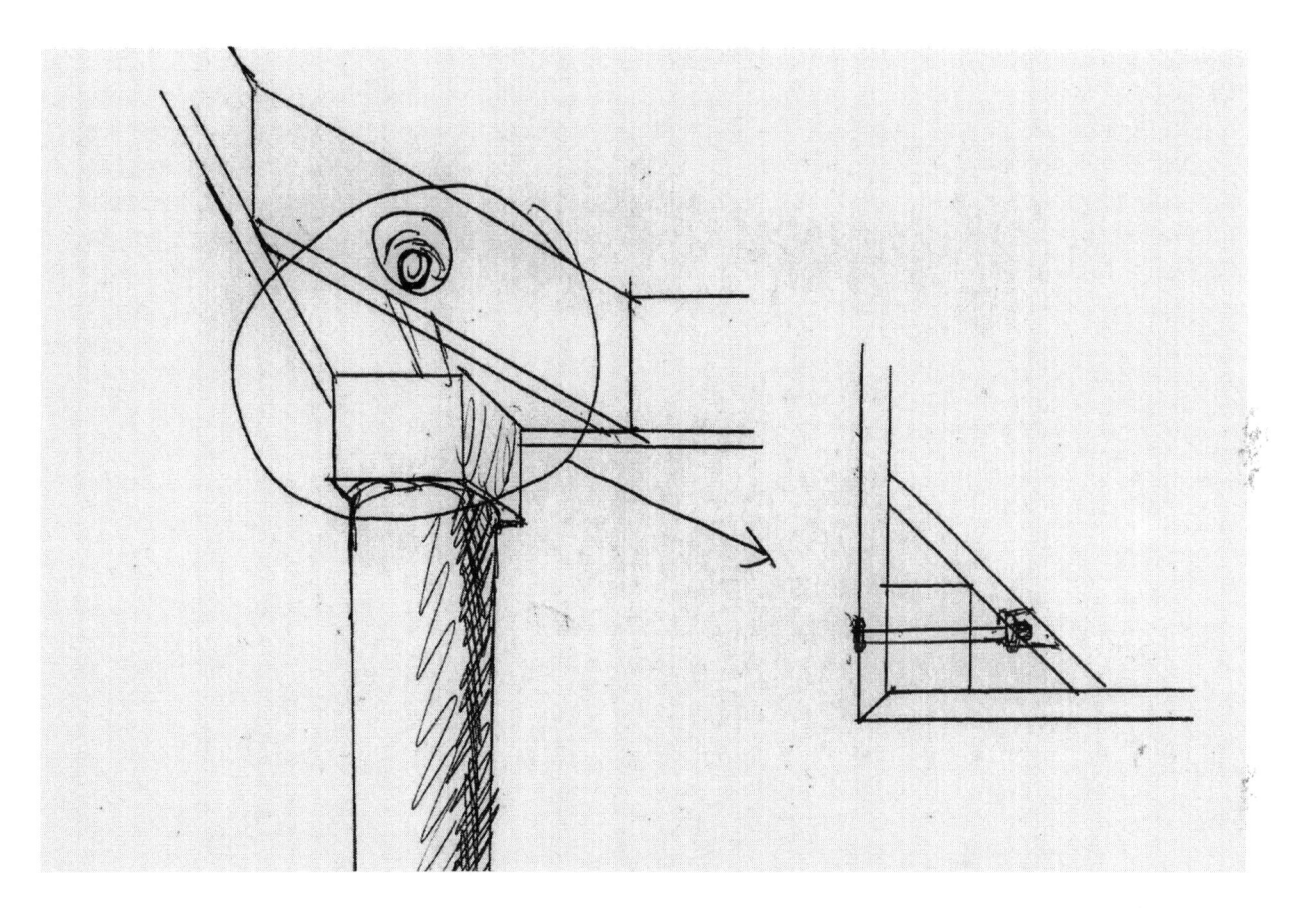

Figure Three: The proper installation of the bolt, fastening the top of the leg to the table

Notice that in Figure Three above, the bolts are run in criss cross over each other and you want to conceal them as much as possible. You also want to fasten the wing-nut on the inside of the table, so people who sit near a leg won't snag their clothing on the bolt.

Now that you have made the dining room table, it's time to make the chairs which match the table. Dining room chairs are special. The are not simple ordinary chairs. These chairs are to be elegant and clearly understood by everyone who comes into your house that they are only for special occasions. When it comes to making the chairs, you will want to use the same wood as you did for the table. It is important that the wood of the table and the chairs match.

Making the chairs for your dining room set can be done in a variety of ways. The first thing you need to think about is the seat. Do you want upholstery for the seat or do you want the traditional hard wood seat. The latter would be simpler to craft, though you will learn some upholstery in this chapter.

Typically, a chair is made with wood which can sometimes be bent. There is a special technique to bend wood without breaking it. You have to steam it. Basically, you need to build a form which you need to fasten the wood on. This is done in an area where you can have immense amounts of steam, like a steam bath, so to speak. What happens, moisture makes the wood pliable. For example, have you noticed that you can bend a live tree branch to a point? This is the same concept here. You need to build a container large enough for the pieces of wood which will become the back support of the chair. You can make this box of wood ahead of time. Place this wood inside and then steam it up for a few hours.

While steaming the wood, you want to fashion a jig with some thick plywood as the supports and 2X4s to fasten the wood to. You can see how this is done in Figure Four below. You may have to repeat this process several times until the wood has come to its desired shape. You may want to first use rope and pulleys to bend the plank, then get vices of different sizes to force the wood into shape. When you make the jig, you should have several 2X4s fastened together on the bottom of the jig and a couple of 2X4s or a 4X4 on the top to push down the wood with the vices.

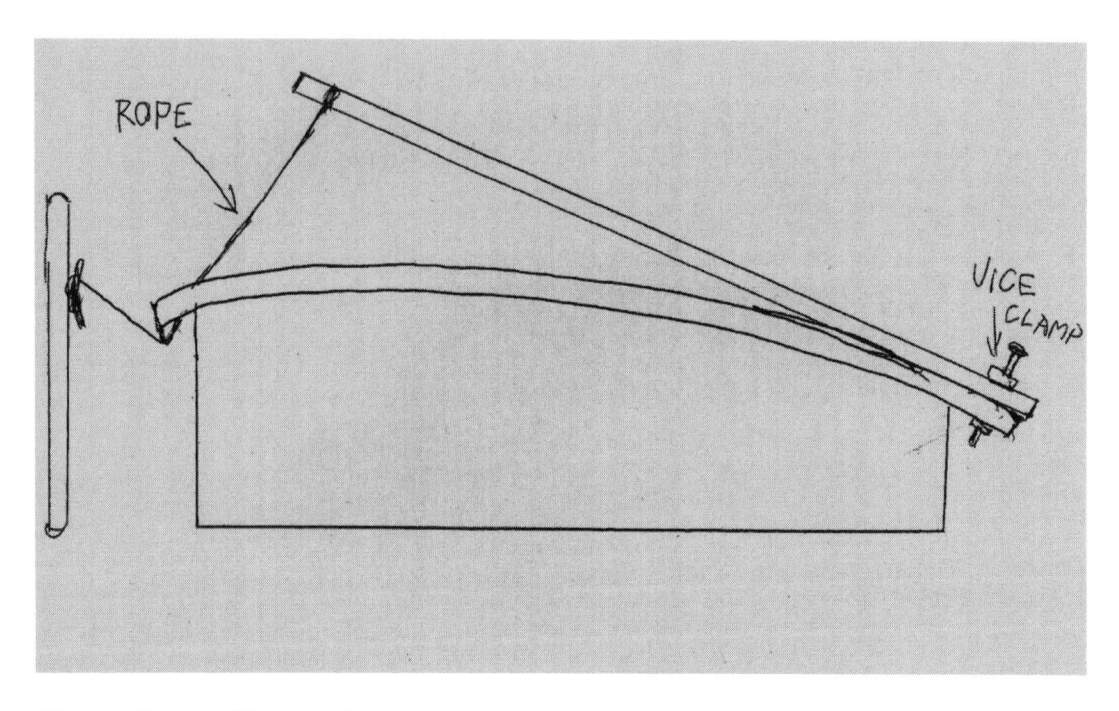

Figure Four: Shaping jig
Notice in Figure Four above how the wood needs to be placed on top of the jig. You also need to remember that once you have taken the wood out of the steamer, it will be very moist. As you place it on the jig, you want to have the wood out in the sun or in a dry room with heat. You will have to dry the wood before you can apply any paint or finish.

The ideal way to dry the wood after being steamed is to keep it in a well ventilated area and have a couple of kerosene jet heaters running to dry it. Keep the wood in the jig until completely dry to insure it will have the shape you desire.

Once all the wood is ready, you need to have everything organized and you will be ready to assemble the chairs of your dining room set. The first thing you will need to do is to take the back supports and the front legs and form the skeleton of the seat. Basically, the back support posts also function as the back legs of the chair. We recommend that you have one piece of wood be as both the back support and the back leg of the chair to make it stronger.

When making the skeleton of the seat, you want to add some pieces of wood at an angle on each corner as shown in Figure Five below. These add extra support and make sure the chair won't collapse under you or your guests. You can then go ahead with wither upholstery or a wood seat.

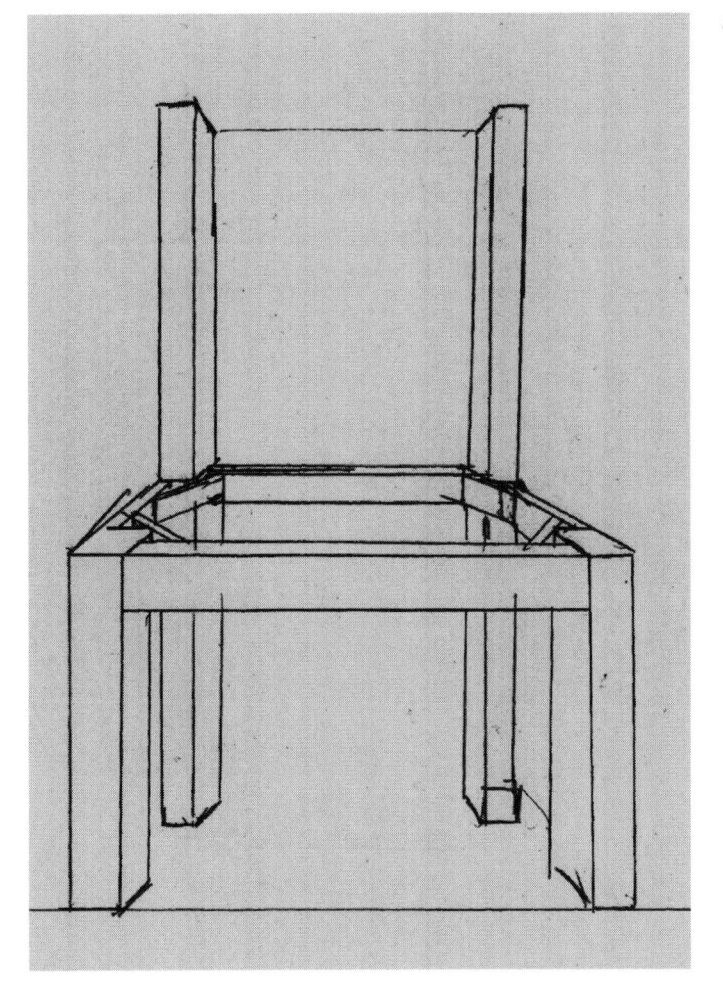

Figure Five: The finished skeletal structure of the seat

Notice how the angled pieces form triangles at each corner. Structurally, triangles are the strongest structures, that is why you want triangles on every corner for the skeleton of both the table and chairs. Once you have finished the skeletal structure of the chairs, you need to decide if you want to have a hard seat or an upholstered seat. In this segment, we will learn how to make a hard seat. Upholstery will be covered in the following segment of this chapter.

Making a hard seat is rather simple. All you need to do is to find a board of the wood the rest of your chair is made of. You cut it to size. It is desirable to cut the seat in a way that it would overlap the skeletal structure a little bit. See Figure Six below. You can make the seat flat or you can engrave the form of the back of your thighs for added comfort. This can simply be done by using corse grit sandpaper to sand the shallow divots into the wood. Then simply use a fine grade sandpaper to smooth it out.

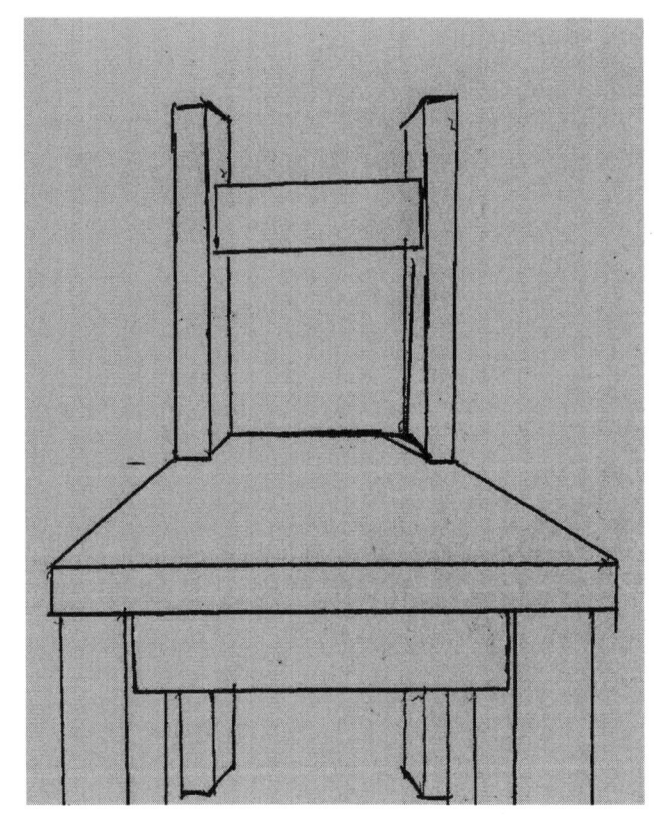

Figure Six: The hard seat installed on the chair

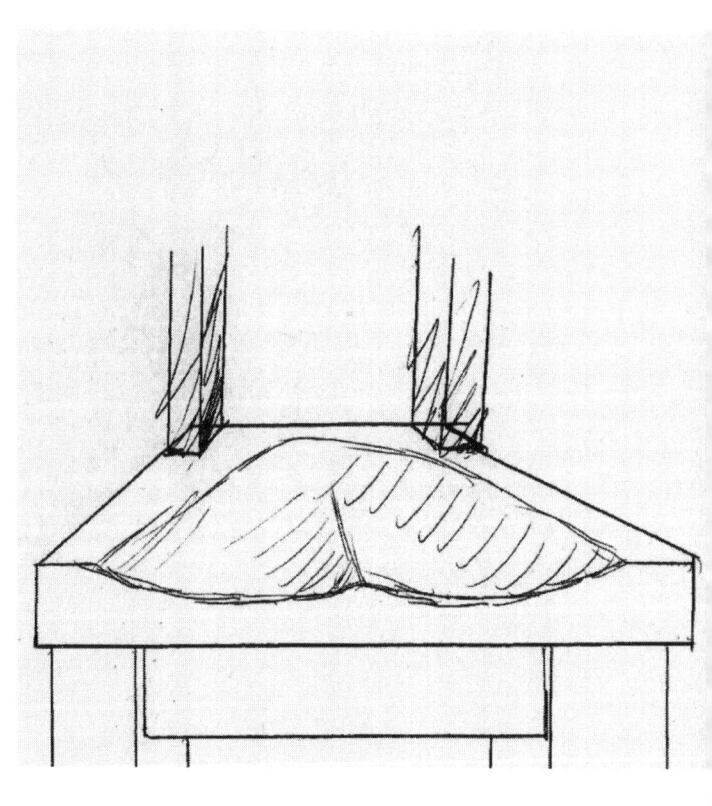

Figure 6a

Figure 6b

Notice in Figure 6a, the seat is flat and this is the easiest to fashion. Figure 6b, on the other hand, shows how the seat would look with the thigh and buttocks divots for added comfort during long periods or sitting at a formal five course meal.

Hard and Upholstered Seats
As mentioned above, with your dining room set, you could have an option of having a hard seat or an upholstered seat. We already explained a bit about hard seats, but we can cover it somewhat in this segment. Hard seats for chairs are the easiest to do and are quicker to make. When fastening a hard seat to your chairs, use a high quality wood adhesive and finish nails.

What is upholstery? Upholstery is basically the art of adding a soft cushioned padding to the seat by using a mixture of heavy duty leather, vinyl, or fabric and padding medium. Typically, the padding in upholstered furniture, such as chair seats is heavy duty foam rubber. Why foam rubber? Well, foam rubber does not come apart easily and will not fall out as much over time as some of the older padding media would.

Cloth used in upholstery can range from heavy duty canvas, denim, or other decorative heavy duty cloth made specifically for upholstery.

Making an upholstered seat for your dining room chairs, or for any other chairs you want to make is rather simple. Take a piece of three quarter inch thick plywood and cut a piece of foam rubber which is up to three inches thick and bevel it around the edges. Foam rubber is easy to cut and if you have a long serrated knife, you can cut it fairly easily.

Use an adhesive to glue the foam rubber padding to the wooden seat. Once the adhesive is dry and the foam rubber is glued to the wooden base of the seat, then take the upholstery cloth of your choice and cut it to overlap at least a couple of inches than the size of the seat. Take the excess cloth and tightly tack it to the bottom of the seat base. Be sure that the cloth is tightly stretched across the foam rubber and use a staple gun to staple the upholstery cloth to the base of the seat.

Fastening the upholstered seat to the chair is also rather easy. All you need to do is add some metal strips which have holes in them. Screw the metal strips to the seat skeleton and then place the upholstered seat on the skeleton and using short wood screws, screw the upholstered seat by the plywood base to the metal strips securely.

Building a Standard Kitchen Table and Chairs
A kitchen table is as much of a necessity as a dining room table, but the difference is that the kitchen table should be used as an everyday eating area and not a formal eating area. In general, kitchen tables and chairs are much smaller than a dining room set. Typically, a kitchen table can be either built into the kitchen as an augment of your countertop or can be a simple round country style table with folding leaves affixed on hinges and can fold out for extra company.

In this segment, we will only cover the construction of the country style kitchen table, as countertops and the like will be covered elsewhere. Making a country style table may have some sentimental memories for some of you. This could have been the table which was in

Grandma's kitchen, or you may have had a country home where you grew up and your parents had this kind of table. The country style table does have that quaint charm and a wonderful addition to your kitchen.

Building the base skeleton and legs of the kitchen table is a bit different from the dining room table we built above. Basically, when building the country style table, you do not need to make the legs removable. The typical country table has the central part of the table about two and a half feet wide, just wide enough to get through most doorways. This means that all you need to do is use a lave, like you did for the dining room table to make the legs. As before, simply keep a good six inches or more as the original square shape the 4X4 originally came as. Likewise, try to cut all the leg pieces the same size before you run it in the lave, but as an added precaution, do not make some decorative features at the very bottom of the legs.

Upon fashioning all four legs, you want to chisel a rectangular hole in two of the sides of the tops of the legs of the table. You then want to take some wood planks and on each end cut a tongue which will fit into the hole that is chiseled into the leg. This is how you assemble the table together, as shown in Figure Seven below.

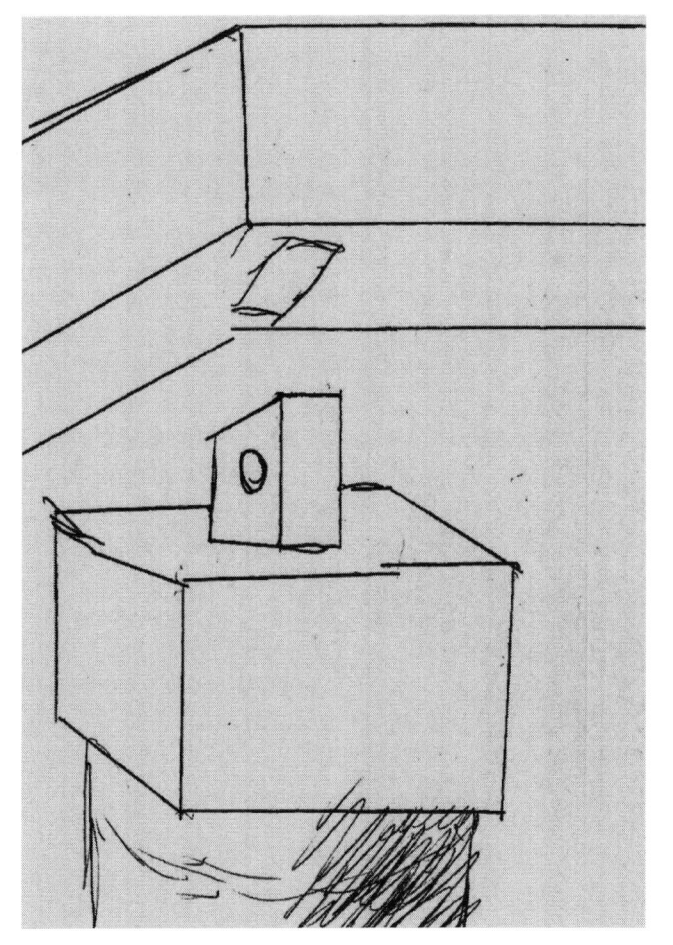

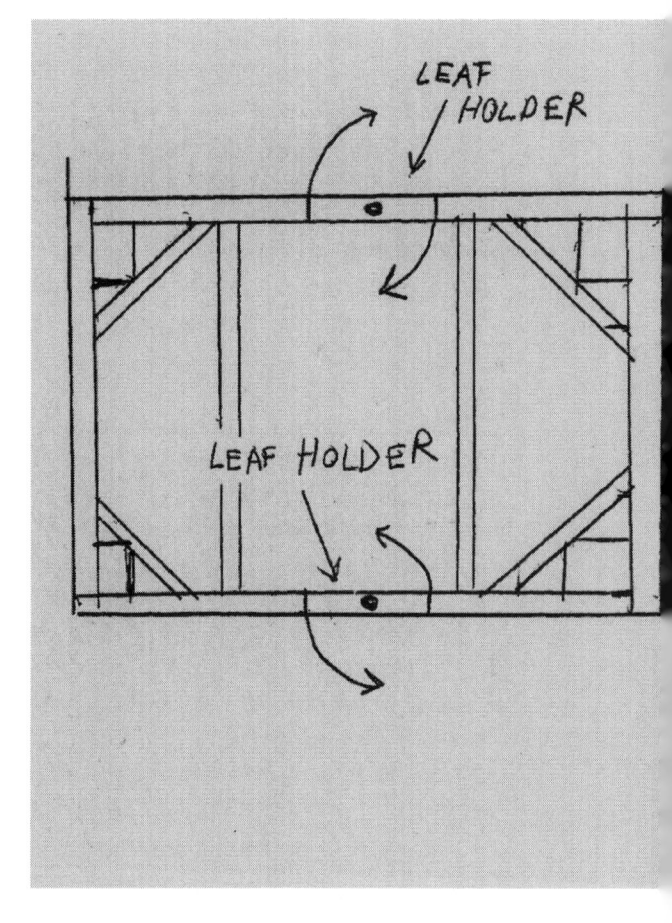

Figure Seven: The basic skeletal structure for the country style table.

Figure 7a

Figure 7b

As seen in Figure 7a above, this is a close up of the hole in the leg and the tongue on the support plank. The tongue should fit tightly into the hole in the leg. You can then bolt the leg and plank together with a permanent bolt, washer, and nut. Recess the bolt and get wood peg tops to mask the bolt head and nut.

Figure 7b, on the other hand, shows the entire table skeletal structure put together. Like you did with the dining room table, you also need to place the diagonal pieces of wood forming a triangle at each corner, to make the structure very strong.

Building the top of the kitchen table is a step-by-step process. Typically, the country style kitchen table is round, so what you need to do is to find good quality wood planking which you can cut into a large circle. You want to cut the circle into thirds. Sometimes, you may have to go to a specialty store or a type of lumber yard which has fine woods specifically made for people who make furniture to find quality wood in such large sizes.

Ideal woods for a country style kitchen table would include aspen, pine, oak, walnut, birch, poplar, or hickory. You can use more expensive woods, such as mahogany or ebony, but typically, those are not woods ideal for a kitchen table. The kitchen table is the main table where you eat your everyday meals, do activities and homework with the kids, or other things. In most households, the kitchen can be the center of activity and often things are done on the kitchen table. Thus, think about that before you spend a fortune on the finer woods which would fit better with a dining room setup.

Assembling the top of the kitchen table should be done first by screwing the hinges on the center part of the table and the folding leaves on either side. Ideally, you want to use piano hinges for the leaves. See Figures Eight and Nine below to see how the leaves get fastened to the central part of the top and how the entire top gets fastened to the legs and top skeleton.

When fastening the skeletal structure for the central part of the table top, you will want to set the top on the floor over some protective cloth or old bedsheets to keep the wood from being scratched by the concrete floor. When making the skeletal structure which is fastened to the legs, you will want to cut notches on the top beams of the long part of the skeletal structure. Make the notches wide enough to screw in 1X2s.

At the same time you will want to have a movable 2X2 on either side of the skeletal structure with a brace under the central 1X2 strut. The 2X2s should be about six to seven inches long. On the outer side of the long support beam you want to get a lock bolt and drill two holes the same diameter as that of the lock bolt. One hole should be at the far end of the 2X2 and the other about four inches from the end. This is the leaf holder. This way, when you need more table room and you want to open the leaf, you can slide the 2X2 and lock it into place so it won't move and the leaf won't slam down on you.

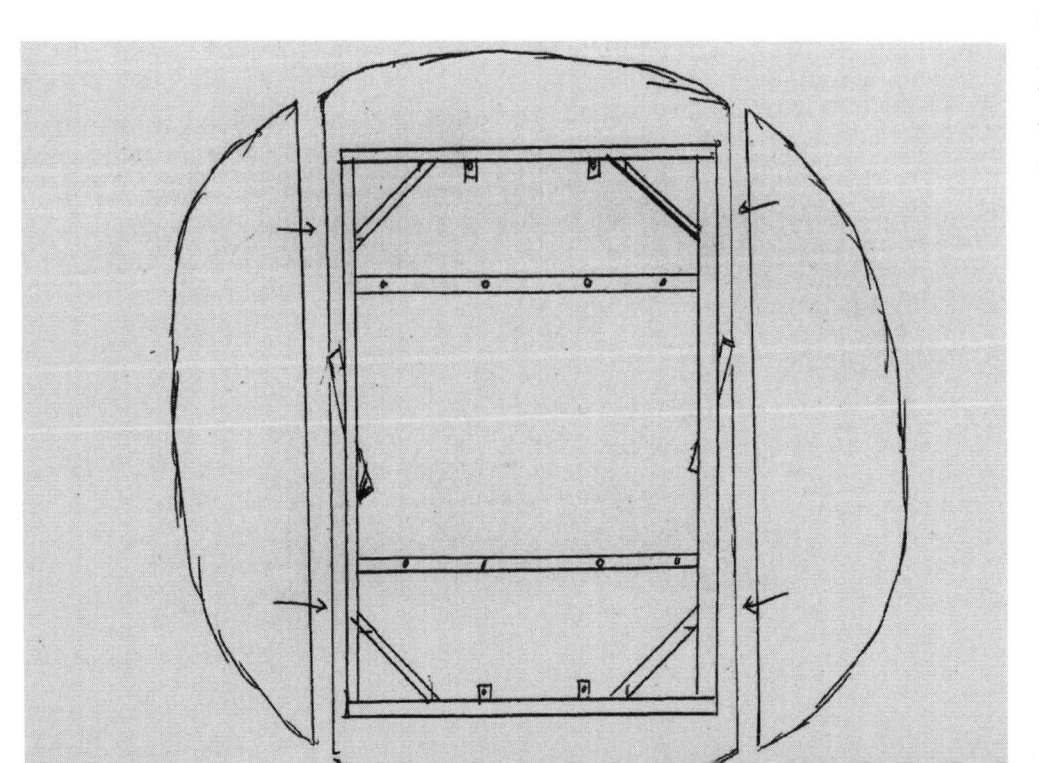

Figure Eight: Attaching the folding leaves to the central part of the table top

Notice above in Figure Eight how the leaves get fastened together with the center of the table top and then you have the entire table top put together. You can use other hinges if you don't like to use piano hinges, but we believe that piano hinges are the best because they are a single hinge for the entire leaf. They can be a bit more difficult to install than two or three smaller hinges but they are stronger. Piano hinges do come in different lengths so you want to measure the length of the seam before you buy them. The piano hinge should be at least three quarters of the length of the seam between the folding leaf and the center of the table. Ideally, the piano hinge should be placed in the middle with the same length of space from the edge of the hinge to the edge of the table.

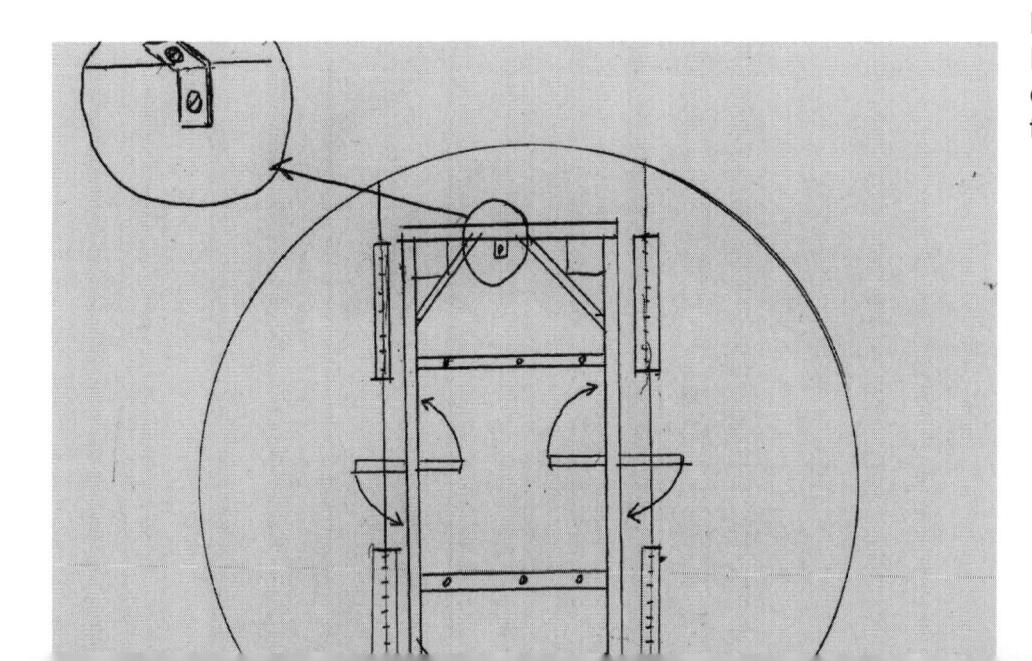

Figure Nine: Fastening the base of the table to the table top

Notice in Figure Nine, the under side of the top should be screwed onto the struts fashioned from a series of 1X2s. Use short screws which will not penetrate the table top. Once you have done this, install the slider leaf supports and the lock bolts. That's it, you're done and you can turn it on its feet and add your desired finish to it.

Note that making the kitchen chairs use the same concept as making those of the dining room table, just on a smaller scale. In the next segment, you will learn how to make bar stools and you can learn how to make different back supports which you can apply to your kitchen chairs as well.

Building Bar Stools
Building bar stools is a bit different from building chairs. In general, bar stools do not have a back support like chairs do, and those that do have one, it is much lower than that of a chair. Bar stools are also much higher than a chair.

Building a bar stool is also much simpler than building a chair. Simply take a large piece of wood which is about two to three square feet and cut it into a circle, so you have the seat. At the bottom of the seat, simply drill four holes which are about an inch in diameter. See Figure Ten below.

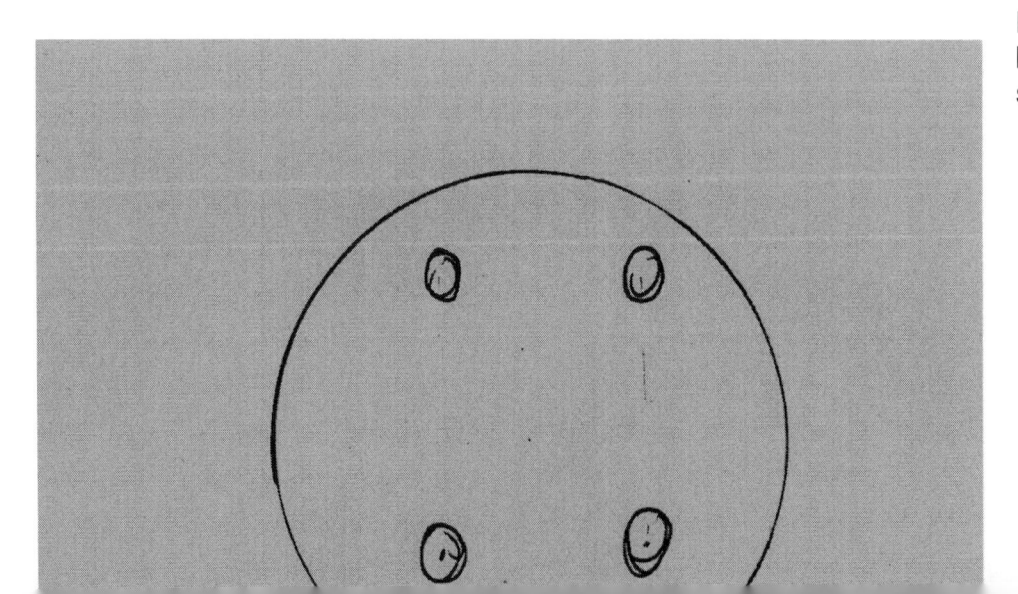

Figure Ten: The bottom of the bar stool seat

Notice how the holes are drilled in the bottom. There is no need to have the holes drilled all the way through. Just enough to drive in the legs. You also want to make the holes at a slight diagonal so the legs taper down so the feet of the legs are wider than the tops of the legs.

Making the legs for the bar stool can be a bit tricky. You need to take 2X2s for this job and then you can simply make the peg which will fit into the holes by sawing the corners off at the top, as shown in Figure Eleven below. Use a wood chisel to fine tune the pegs when you are finished with the legs. You will also want to drill two holes on two of the sides of the legs to add some support struts to make the stool sturdy. You can run the legs through a lave to make them round or you can keep them square, which ever is your personal taste. Then in Figure Twelve, see how the finished product will look.

Figure Eleven: The completed bar stool

Notice how the bar stool looks completed. To add a small back support, the thing you need to do is drill holes in the seat on one side for at least four or five small posts which are about one foot high. Then you want to take a top piece of wood to place on the top of the wooden struts. This can be difficult and you will have to steam the wood in a jig to bend them into shape.

Andirondak Chairs
What are Andirondak chairs? Well, these are basically the wooden deck recliners you see most people have. These chairs are easier to make than the ones mentioned above and also have a separate foot rest which can be used to enjoy the sunset if you have them on a deck which faces a lake or the ocean.

Building the Andirondak chairs requires heavy pressure treated wood. These are basically intended to be deck furniture. These are primarily recliners which are not adjustable. These chairs come in two parts, the chair and the foot rest. You want to start with the chairs.

Start with the chairs, as they are the most difficult to construct. The materials you will need to build the Andirondak chairs are listed below.

A. **Pressure treated wood** or fine hard woods which can handle the elements. Typically, Andirondak chairs are made from either pressure treated yellow pine, or the more expensive models can be made from redwood or cedar. The wood is important as it has to be hard and capable of handling all the punishment mother nature will throw at the chairs, especially if you live in the northern climates. The cut of wood you will need for the Andirondak chairs need to be 2X8s for the structure, 1X4s for the slats on the back support and 1X2s for the seat.
B. **Linseed oil** to preserve the wood. Like your deck planking, the sun can be the worst enemy of your Andirondak chairs. As wood gets exposed to the sun, it tends to crack and parch the wood if it is not oiled.

C. **Stains** can be an option if you don't like working with linseed oil. Stains can also add color to your wood. There are special stains you can get which are made especially for treated and outdoor wood.
D. **Wood bolts and eight penny self drilling wood screws** to put the parts of the Andirondak chair together. Basically, the wood bolts are used to fasten the larger pieces which make the skeleton of the chair and the wood screws are used to fasten the planks to the chair. Self drilling wood screws boar deep into the wood and anchor themselves in the wood, thus they are less likely to pop up and tear your clothing or cut you as you are sitting in the chair.

Building the chair skeleton can be a bit tricky. Since Andirondak chairs are deck recliners, the back support needs to be leaning back at least at a 50 degree angle, likewise, the seat needs to be a 50 degree angle. This allows you to be able to sit back and relax. Take the 2X8s and using your miter saw, simply cut the proper angles and build the seat first, then build the basic structure for the back support.

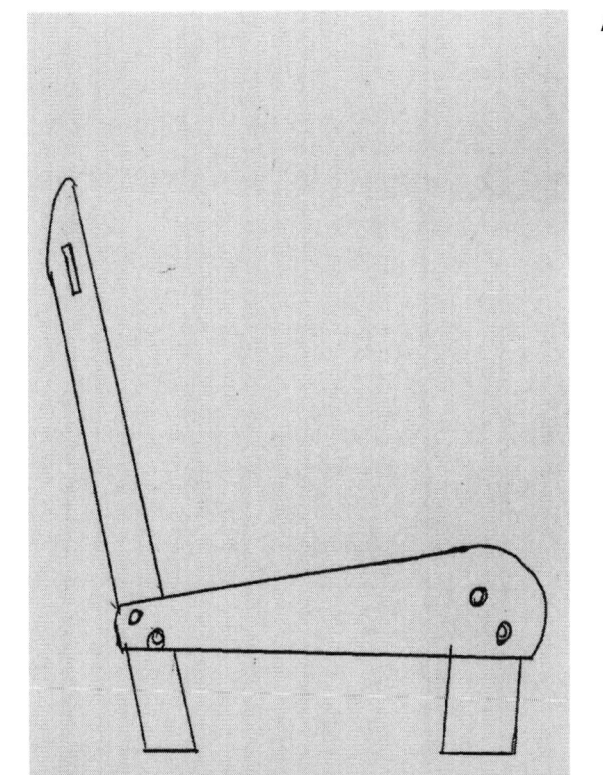

Figure Twelve: Building the skeleton of the Andirondak chair

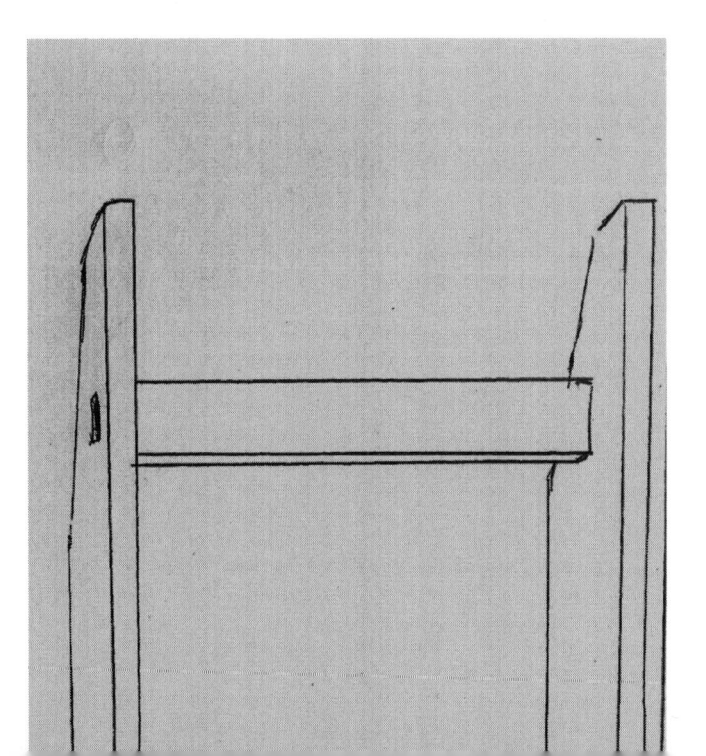

Figure 12a   Figure 12b

Notice in Figure 12a, the basic skeletal structure of the seat seems rather simple. You want to add the back support posts to the structure and use basic 2X4s between the back posts to hold the 1X4 slats which make the back support of the chair, shown in Figure 12b.

When attaching the back support slats, you will need to take the 1X4s and cut them to fit accordingly. The typical Andirondak chair usually has a rounded top of the back support. You can drill a small pilot hole or two in each slat and temporarily drive a nail in so you can pull it out later, and then mark where you will need to cut the 1X4s. Use a jigsaw to cut them then screw them into their proper space as seen in Figure Fourteen below.

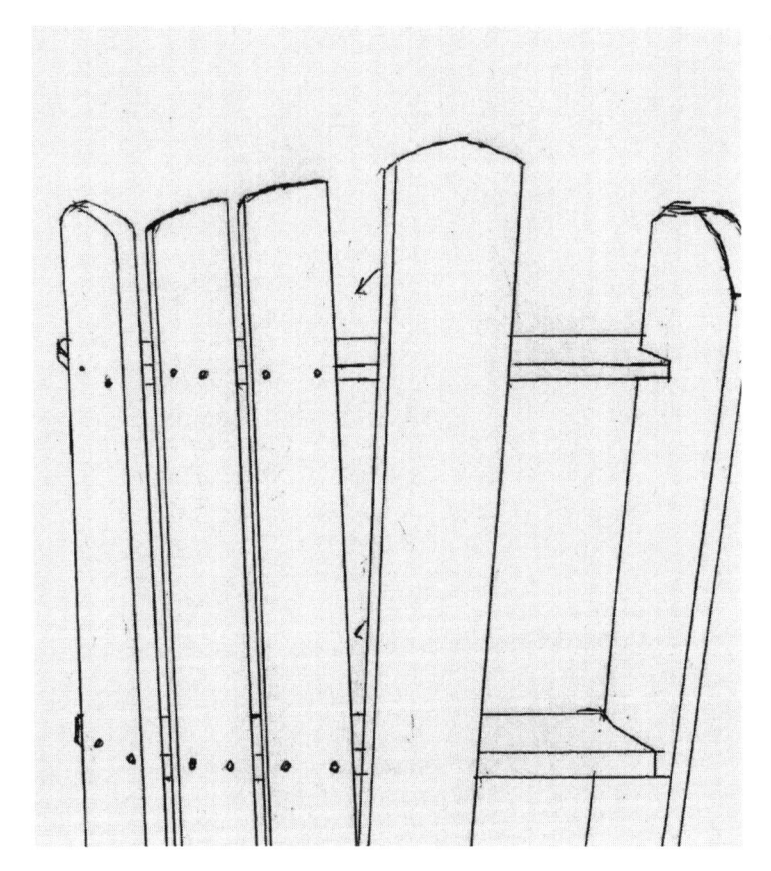

Figure Thirteen: The back support of your Andirondak chair completed

Notice how the back supports of your Andirondak chair round up to the top on both sides, making a small semicircle for your back support.

Making the slats for the seat is very simple. All you need to do is simply take the 1X2s and cut them down to size and screw into the wood supports of the skeletal structure. See Figure Fifteen below to see the completed seat.

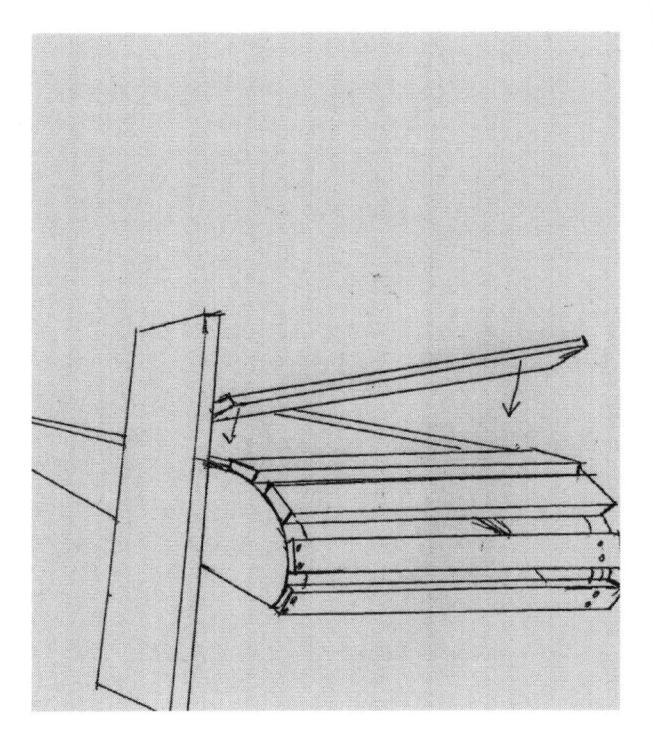

Figure Fourteen: Installing the slat which make the seat

After completing the Andirondak chair, you now need to make the footrest. What is the purpose of the foot rest? Basically, the foot rest is designed to help you recline. Basically, you sit back in the Andirondak chair and then extend out your legs and have your feet rest on the foot rest, you feel comfortable and relaxed on that warm summer night.

Making the footrest is not as difficult as making the chair. Basically, all you need to do is simply take the same 2X8s which are left over from the Andirondak chair and cut them to an angle which runs opposite of the angle of the seat on the Andirondak chair. Simply screw on the 1X2 slats across the footrest as you have done with the seat.

Figure Fifteen: The completed Andirondak chair

Building a Front Porch Swing
A front porch swing can be pleasant when you have an old home or even a newer home and you can enjoy the front porch during the warm summer months. Typically, the porch swing is considered a permanent fixture as it is suspended from the ceiling of the porch with chains. The items you will need to build a front porch swing are listed below.

A. **2X4s** to build the skeletal structure of the swing
B. **Chains** to hang the swing to the ceiling beam of the porch
C. **1X2s** to make the slats for the back support and seat

You want to begin by making the skeletal structure of the porch swing. Think of it like building a bench. While building the skeletal structure, you will want to also think about installing eye bolts on which the chain will be coupled to.

Before coupling the chains to the bench, you will want to attach the 1X2s to the back support first, then make the seat. Your best bet with the seat is to screw on the 1X2s length wise versus vertically like for the back support.
Suspending the porch swing can be a two or three man jog. Before actually coupling the chains, you want to make sure the ceiling where you plan to hang the bench is strong enough to support the weight. You will want to couple one chain on each armrest and on each side of the back support. Then couple the three chains in the center and hang from the ceiling. That's all there is to it.

In this chapter you basically learned how to make tables and different kinds of chairs. You will learn more advanced projects as you keep reading through this book.

Chapter Seven

Hanging Doors and Windows

You've probably decided to get this book because you have an old house and you want to do a lot of the remodeling yourselves. Maybe, you want to have customized windows and doors for your home to have that unique look which only you have in mind. Whatever the reason, you will need to know how to hang windows and doors. You might also need to learn how to make windows and doors, however, you need know about the problems with wooden window frames and what the benefits are of using vinyl windows as a better alternative to wood from the elements. Some of the things you will learn in this chapter are listed below.

A. **Hanging doors** with basic hinges. The difficulty of hanging a door may seem more daunting than it seems. This can be done very simply, however, it is a project which might require several people to help you lift the door into place.
B. **Making floating panel doors** for your bedroom and other rooms for your home. These kinds of doors are ideal for those of you who have an old Victorian home and knowing this skill and doing this project can help you restore the original character of your old home.
C. **Making French doors** for that special room. French doors are nice for say a parlor, living, or dining area linked to another room. The nice thing about French doors is that if you have them inside your home and they are added to a room with a lot of sunlight, they will let the sunlight into other parts of the house
D. **Hanging a sliding barn door** can be great for those of you who have a large home out in the country or have converted an old barn into a home, this can be neat addition to your decor.
E. **The basics of windows** and what you need to know about making and hanging windows. You will also learn how to restore old original windows which might be difficult to replace
F. **Double hung windows** and how to both maintain and repair them. One of the most frustrating types of window construction when it comes to windows. Learn how to fix and make double hung windows.
G. **Alternatives to double hung windows** can be much easier to deal with and maintain than the traditional double hung window. Basically, there are only a few countries which regularly use double hung windows because of their high maintenance. Besides the US and Canada, double hung windows can also be seen in housing construction in the UK and Australia. Learn how to make sliding windows, hinged windows, and multi-opening windows.
H. **The best woods** for outdoor windows and doors and how to properly treat them. You will learn about mastic and what it is used for. Also learn about different finishes designed to handle the elements.

Hanging Doors
Anytime you remodel a room, you may have to refurbish a door, replace a door, or even refinish a door. Whatever the reason, you will have to learn how to hang a door properly so it won't sag

and scrape the floor. The biggest problem with doors is that they are heavy. This is why this should be a project for two or three people. Never attempt to hang a door yourself, as you could take out your back out because a door is heavy and an awkward shape which can overstrain your back.

Removing an existing door for renovation can simply be done by removing the hinge pins from the hinge sockets. Then simply remove the door from its jam. It's that simple. Most door hinges are made so you can remove the hinge pins. Older doors which may have several coats of paint may be impossible to remove the hinge pin, thus in that case you may have to remove the hinge all together. Removing a hinge with multiple layers of paint can also be a challenge, as the old coats of paint my have covered the driver slots in the tops of the screws, so you may have to take a knife to scrape the paint out of the slots before you can get a screwdriver in there to remove the screw.

Dealing with tough coats of paint can be an issue in older homes when wanting to remove a door for renovation or replacement. When this is the case, you can use a strong paint thinner to help remove some of the older coats of paint. You also have to remember that older homes might contain alkyd paints containing lead. These paints are now illegal and you may have to hire a hazmat crew to remove those paints.

Having removed the door from its jam, it is now time to refurbish it. Basically, depending on the kind of finish is on the door, you will have to sand it down. If the door was finished with varnish and stains, then sanding comes easy. Simply use a corse grit sandpaper and then fine grit when you have removed all the varnish and most of the stain. You need to understand that removing stains can be difficult as most stains sink into the pores of the wood.

When stripping the doors from years of paint and bringing back the old beauty of the natural wood the door was made from, you may need to get paint thinners first. Typically, the older the house is, the more the likelihood you will need paint thinners. You will also have to scrape the old paints off with a paint scraper, which you can get at any hardware or home improvement store. Try first, however, to remove the paint without the paint thinner. Typically, older paints and primers tend to peal off, so sometimes, you may find the right place and large swaths of paint will come off. Then use the paint thinner to remove the more stubborn areas of the old paint.

Hanging the door back up is much like having taken it down. Make sure the hinges fit together and put the pins back in place. When building a new home or room, and when placing a new door, you typically want to have three sets of hinges. One at the bottom, one at the middle, and one on top. This will ensure the door is firmly placed and won't fall when pivoting open and closed.

Making Floating Panel Doors
Making floating panels can be a bit tricky, but if you have an older house and want to create that feel of antiquity and restore the character of that house, then you will want to make the floating panel doors.

What exactly are floating panel doors? Basically, the best way to explain what a floating panel door is the kind of door shown in Figure One below.

Figure One: The typical floating panel door

Notice above in Figure One, the panels in parts of the door. Basically, the floating panel door is a door composed of wooden slats with panels floated in grooves of the slats. The panels are also beveled to give that look of a classic door.

Making the door can be difficult, but with the right power tools and skills learned here, it can be a fairly simple project.

Basically, you will want to make the lower part of the door first. Make the panels by buying panels made from a fine wood which is about three quarters of an inch thick. Cut out a tongue on all four sides of the panel and bevel all the sides by plaining the corners of the edges on each side of the tongue as seen in Figure Two below.

Figure Two: The actual panel

After making all the panels using the technique shown above in Figure Two, you can start making the slats of the door. Depending on the complexity of the door you want to make, most floating panel doors have four to six floating panels, either just two large panels or two large panels and two small panels at the top.

When making the slats which basically are the brunt of the door structure, you want to fashion a larger tongue on the ends of the vertical slats. The middle slats should have a groove carved out that will snugly fit into the tongue of the panels. Likewise, the end slats on the sides, top, and bottom should have a groove which corresponds to the panel's tongue on the inside. See Figure Three below to see how the floating panels fit into the grooves.

Figure Three: Assembling the floating panel door

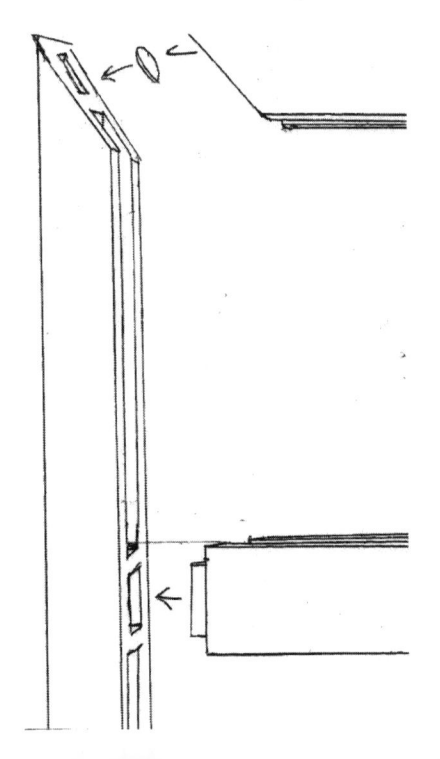

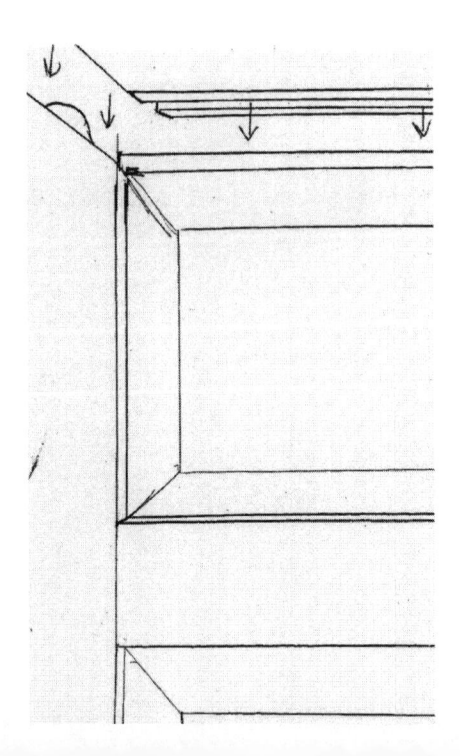

Figure 3a   Figure 3b

Figure 3a shows how the slats of the door get put together and Figure 3b show how the panels get put into the slats. You will want to start with the bottom up. This basically means that Take the bottom slat and then add the bottom panels and tap everything in with a rubber mallet. Use a wood adhesive for the tongs of the slats but do not glue the panels. The panels are intended to float inside and go with the flow as the wood expands and contracts, which wood tends to do over time. You can see the finished product below in Figure Four below.

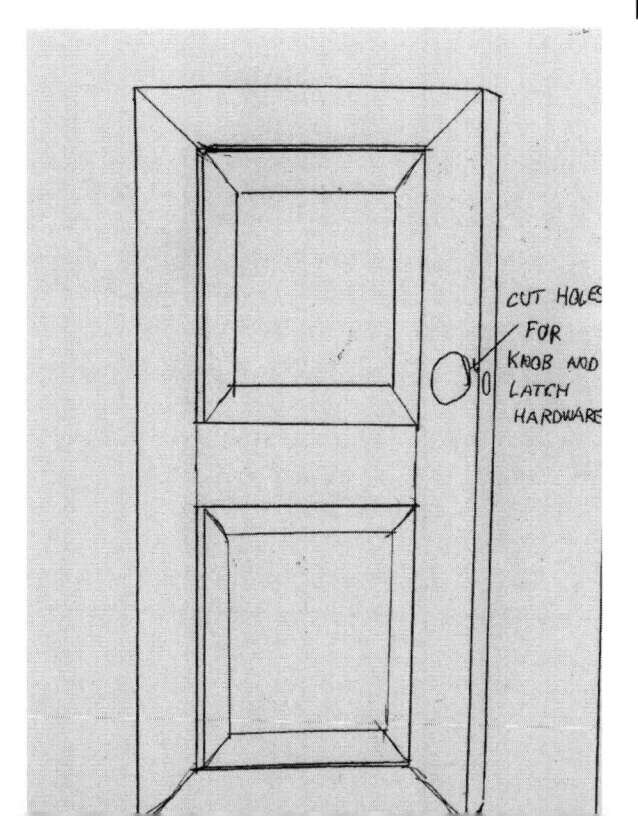

Figure Four: The finished door

Installing the hardware is probably the easiest part. You want to make sure the side slats are fairly wide and are at least an inch thick. When adding the basic door knob, found in most hardware and home improvement stores, you will want to cut a round hole at hand height. You then want to bore a hole on the side of the door big enough to fit the latch of the knob. Then the process is simple. All you will need to do is install the latch and the components of the knob and test the mechanics.

Hinges are also fairly easy. Simply use a router and a jig to carve a notch big enough for the hinges on the door and the door jam. Make sure they correspond with each other. Then take the hinges apart and screw them both onto the door and the door jam. With a couple of friends, simply hang the door by placing it into the hinges and slide in the pins.

Making French Doors
French doors are not really French, but are quite common in France, hence the name. What are French doors? Basically, French doors are large double doors which have glass squares in them to let in a lot of light. French doors can be difficult to make because of the glass squares which need to be placed.

Getting started with making the French doors you will need several of the following materials and tools listed below.

A. **Pieces of 1X1s** to fashion the grid work in which the glass squares need to be placed. These will have to be tongue and grooved to fit the pieces of glass in.
B. **1X6s** for the tops and sides of the French doors
C. **1X12s** for the bases of the French doors
D. **Fancy door knob hardware** and the corresponding locking hardware for the doors.
E. **Locking bolts** if you are making a set of double French doors (Recommended for maximum effect in esthetics.)
F. **Glass** should be purchased at a glass specialty place. You may want to contemplate having the glass warehouser precut all the squares for you. Order a few spares incase you break some when installing them. If you really want to get fancy with your French doors, you can even order the glass to be precut and bevelled if you go to the right merchandiser.
G. **A router and jig** are needed to groove the individual 1X1 pieces for the grid work
H. **A hand and power miter saw** are needed to cut the pieces. The frame pieces can be cut with a power miter saw, but the 1X1s for the grid work may be better cut with a fine toothed hand miter saw as this can be delicate work.
I. **A strong wood adhesive** which will not come apart when glued together.

Making the frames for the French doors is done with the 1X12 at the base of the door, and then using a miter saw, you want to cut the angle of both sides of the 1X12 and 1X6s so that the seam of the corner of the 1X12 and 1X6 is flush. You will have to realize that the width if a 1X6 is about half that of a 1X12. Cut accordingly. The best way to do this is by overlaying the 1X6 over the 1X12 and draw a 45 degree angle across the 1X6. You can then cut the 1X6 first then with the cut 1X6, draw the same line to cut off the corner of the 1X12.   See Figure Five below.

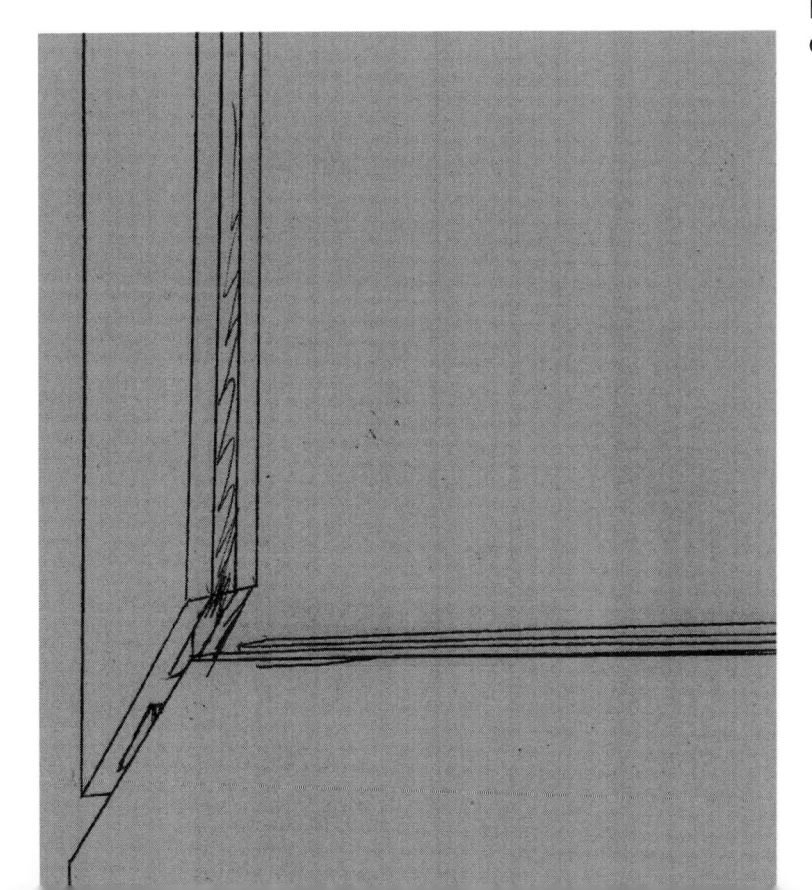

Figure Five: Assembling the base of the French doors

Notice the groove throughout the entire inside of the 1X6s and 1X12s? This is imperative because you need a groove to hold the glass squares and the 1X1s which hold the glass in place.

Installing the grid work and glass squares is the most tedious part of the project. This part needs to be done layer by layer. When making the first row of squares, you will need to take two 1X1s and have a groove in one side of them. Using brads and a strong wood adhesive, you want to glue the 1X1s back to back. The first 1X1s which are placed vertical need to have tongues carved out on the bottom to fit into the groove of the 1X12. Make sure you take accurate measurements before making the doors to make sure the glass squares have an even fit. Any slight mistake may cause the glass not to be snugly in place and fall out.

Always use adhesive when installing the wood pieces of the grid work. Do not attempt to glue the glass to the wood. The glass squares need to float in place, much like the floating panels of a door. Same concept, but on a more delicate scale. See Figure Six below to see how to install the first row of glass squares.

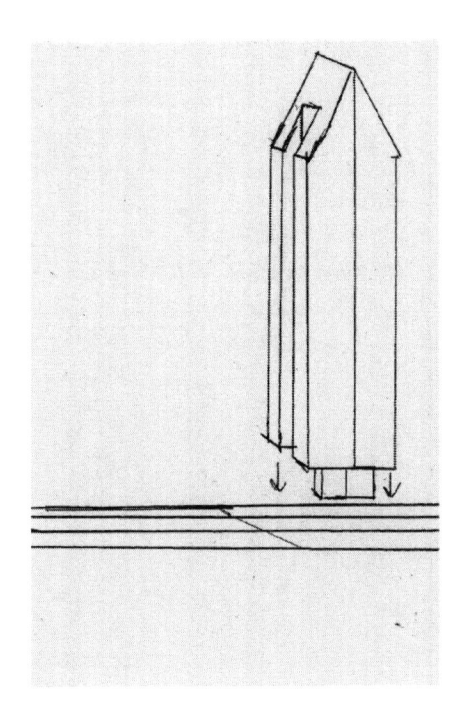

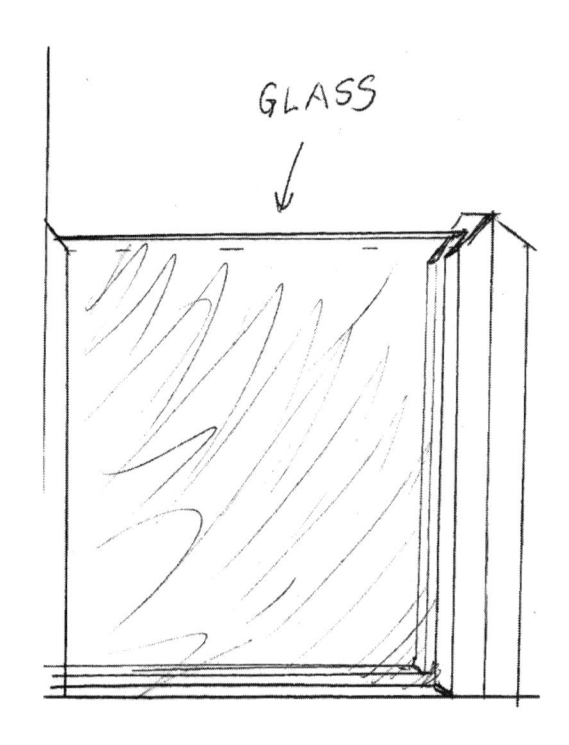

Figure Six: The proper installation of the base line of glass squares
        Figure 6a   Figure 6b

You should attach the two 1X1s together back to back and slide the tongues of the two into the groove of the base 1X12, as shown in Figure 6a. Repeat the process for every square in a horizontal row. Then, as shown in Figure 6b, simply slide the glass squares into the grooves and make sure they fit snugly. The French doors in this example uses beveled glass, as it does give a more classy look to your French doors. You will want to measure everything first to make sure it all fits together when you are ready to install the glass.

After having installed the square glass pains in the base row, you will have to prepare the 1X1s for the rest of the rows until you get to the top. Basically, this can be the more difficult part of the process. When installing the base line of the glass squares, you want to make sure that the top of the glass squares do get in line with the points of the mitered cuts of the 1X1s, as seen above in Figure 6b. This will allow the 1X1s which are placed horizontally will fit snugly.

Use a strong wood adhesive to glue the 1X1s to the vertical 1X1s. The glass will provide the tongue for the grooves in the 1X1s.

Like the vertical 1X1s, glue two 1X1s together back to back and have 45 degree miter cuts on both ends. Do the same thing with the vertical 1X1s and use a small brad to fasten them together before installing the glass. See Figure Seven below. Simply repeat the process until you get to the top.

Figure Seven: Installation of the glass squares above the initial base row

Figure 7a

Figure 7b

Notice in Figure 7a, the 1X1s glued and fastened together with some small brads need to be placed in the mitered areas. Use care in placing the brads to avoid any of the glass squares from breaking. Figure 7b shows how you install the vertical 1X1s and simply repeat this process until you get to the top.

Doing the top of the French doors is the most tricky part of the individual doors. Basically, you want to make sure that the sides and the top part of the French doors are mitered before you begin putting them together. When you have the top row done, you will notice that the tops of the glass squares in line with the tops of the tongues of the 1X1s and partially in line with the 1X6 side parts of the doors. Carefully place the top 1X6 above the last row and gently tap into the 1X6 until it is snug with the glass and the rest of the wood parts. You may have to tap the 1X6 into place with a rubber mallet, but do it gently to prevent any of the glass squares from shattering or cracking and also to keep the fragile grid work from coming apart. See Figure Eight below.

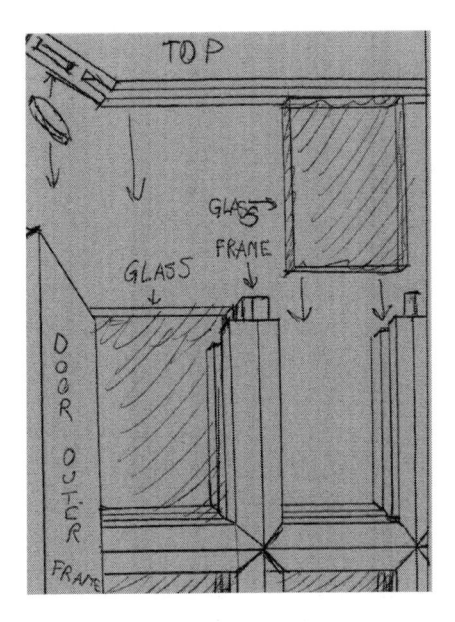

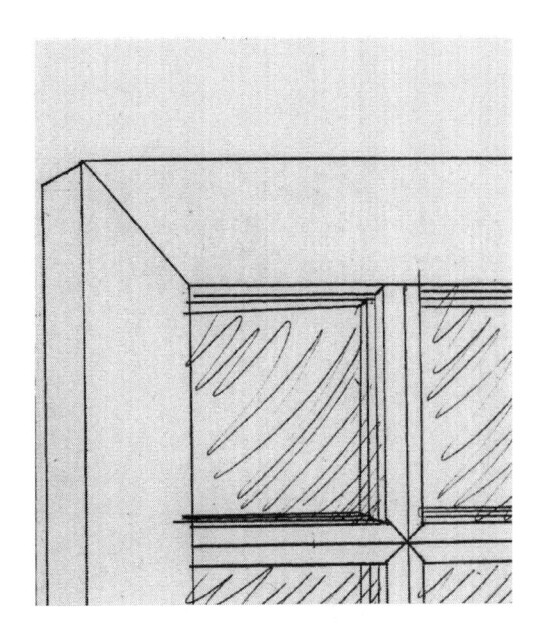

Figure Eight: The top row of glass squares and the top 1X6 board to complete the doors
  Figure 8a   Figure 8b

Notice that the top is the final cap which holds everything in place. You want to have everything secure to hold the doors together. You may also want to place a rabbit wedge inside the mitered corners of the 1X6s and the 1X12 on each door. The rabbit wedge is a flat football shaped piece of wood which can be placed into a groove and with some adhesive, you will have a much stronger bond.

Locking the non-mechanical door is rather simple. You need to remember only one door is mechanical, which means that only one door has the knob and the locking mechanism. The other door needs to be locked into place using manual locking bolts. You can get the basic lock bolts and place one on the top and one on the bottom, but you can also get special locking bolts which are flat and you can use them to lock the door into place and they are flush with the side of the door.

Figure Nine: The finished product.

Notice how nice the French doors are. Places where French doors work the best include an area where there is a lot of sunlight and the adjacent room would be dark with a solid door or areas, such as a divider between your kitchen and dining room or living area and dining room. French doors are also nice as a divider between your dining room and a formal parlor or sitting area. You can also incorporate French doors with a glass wall by making panels the same way as you made the French doors.

Hanging a Sliding Barn Door

If you are the redneck and love country, then this segment is for you. Where do we need a sliding barn door? Well, on a barn, right? Well, yes, you can, but if you want that rustic look to your house and you have the space, then you can even hang one in your own home for that rustic look.

A sliding barn door can also be ideal for those of you who have converted an old barn into your own home. You can also use any kind of wood you like for a sliding barn door. If you like the modern look, you can even create a modern looking sliding barn door by making a sheetrock door and painting it minimalist colors, like whites, blacks, or greys.

Beginning the sliding barn door project is rather simple. All you need is some basic hardware, such as a heavy duty hanging door slider and other hardware which is listed below.

A. **The hanging door slider** is a very heavy duty door slider which is equipped with a track and wheels. The wheels have a groove which locks into the track and get affixed to the door. The track is affixed above the door jam and needs to be twice the length of the door.
B. **Heavy duty bolts** which can be used to bolt the track into the door header on the wall and the wheel chassis to the door.
C. **Air compressor and power wrench,** much like those used by auto mechanics to tighten the bolts so they don't get loose.

Purchasing the barn door slider is a specialty item which you might not find at your typical chain home improvement store, like Menard's, Lowe's, or Home Depot. You will find them at farm supply stores which have a variety of farming merchandise, such as barn equipment and like items. Places to look for a barn door slider would be Tractor Supply, Big R, or Rural King. There can be other like stores which also supply farmers with the necessary hardware for barns and other farm out buildings.

Places where a sliding barn door should be installed can vary. You do not want to install this type of door as an outside door or entrance door to your barn home, as it does have too wide a space between the wall and door itself and can allow too much heating or cooling to escape to the outside.

Inside the home, the sliding barn door is deal for an optional divider for two large rooms. For example, if you have a dining room and a large living room which can also be converted into a sleeping are, the sliding barn door is perfect. You can also install a sliding barn door to the front of a pole barn, which is what this type of door is designed for. Some modern architects have incorporated the sliding barn door as a door into a bedroom and created a pocket to make it into an oversized pocket door.

Fastening the slider rail is fairly simple. Use a water level to make sure the slider is level. Any slight slant in the rail can cause it to slide open or closed, as this type of barn door is heavy. Most building codes require a door header to be a 2X8 or 2X12 minimum, however, you will need a stronger support for a doorway which is wider than four feet. In some cases, using a butcher block laminated beam can add extra beauty with the door rail being painted black, which is usually the color they are sold in. We do advise painting the rail and other barn door hardware before affixing it to the wall. See Figure Ten below on how the door rail should be installed.

Figure Ten: Barn door slider rail installed above opening with extra length for the door in open position.

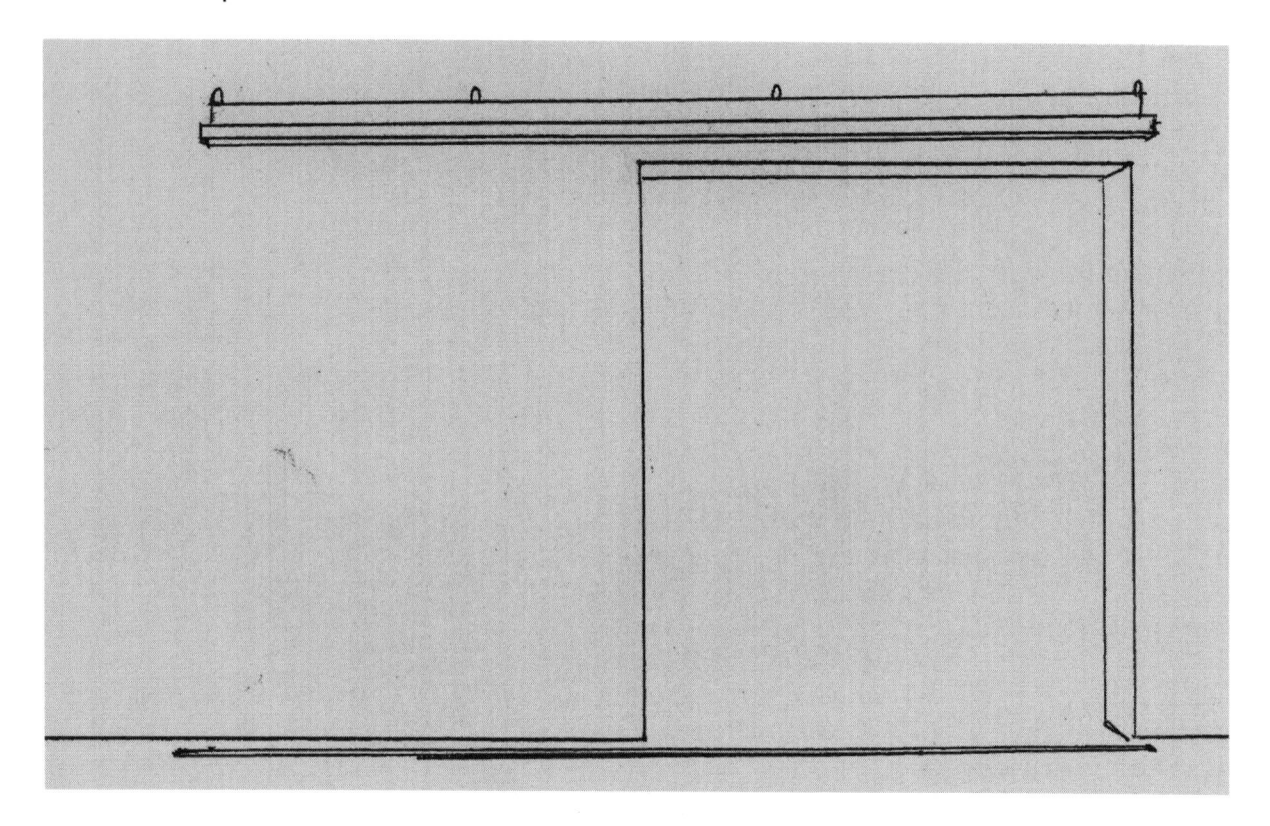

Installing the slider wheel chassis to the top of the door is also fairly simple. Simply follow the directions with the slider track and hardware you purchased. Typically, once you have installed the wheels on the top of the door, it should lock onto the rail once door is lifted into place. See Figure Eleven below.

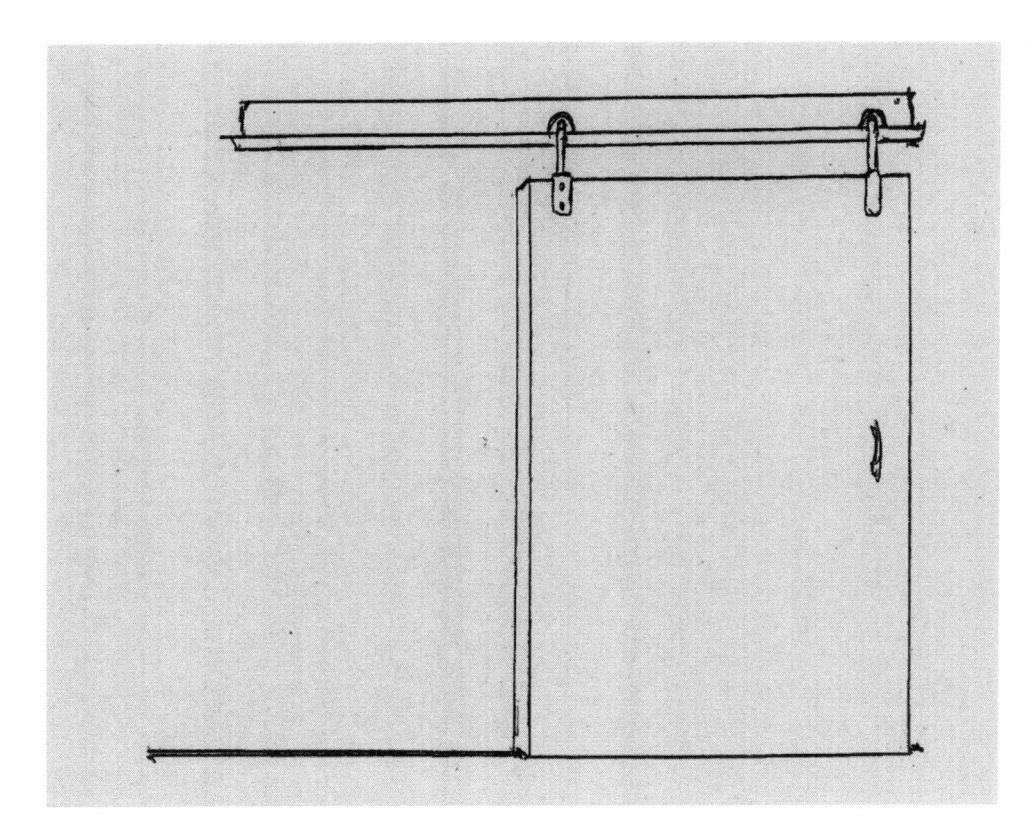

Figure Eleven:
The completed barn door

Remember that sliding barn doors can be very heavy, so when installing them, you want to have at least ten people who are very strong to help you lift it into place and lock the sliding wheels into the overhead track.

The Basics of Windows
Windows are the most difficult woodworking projects to work on. I am sure that many of you have been frustrated with those old wooden double-hung windows which are such a pain to open in the summer after having been closed during those long winter months. The problem with wooden windows is that wood tends to warp. This process can be explained very simply. When wood is exposed to the elements, extreme heat and cold, humidity and dryness, then the wood will expand and contract. This is why it is so important to find the right polyurethane finish or water proof paint for your windows. Likewise, cheaper woods, like pine, tend to warp more than your harder woods, such as oak, teak, or walnut.

Older windows tend to warp because it may have been a while the windows have been refinished or repainted. Older paint, having been exposed to the elements for a long time begins to peal and the primer also begins to peal. This allows the bare wood to be exposed. When you notice the wood is grey and not the color wood should be, it is a sign that it has been exposed to the sun and the elements.

Restoring old windows can be difficult. When wood warps, sometimes it's simply better to replace the entire window. If you have an older home with some curved windows, as is the case with some older Victorian homes, you may want to be very careful not to break the curved glass, as those pains are not mass produced anymore, thus they would have to be custom ordered and that can cost.

Double-Hung Windows
What kinds of windows are double-hung windows? Well, basically, if you live in the United States, Canada, or the UK, you may have double-hung windows in your home. A double-hung window is the typical window with the bottom opening upward. Many people like to get away from these kinds of windows as the older double-hung windows are extremely high maintenance and the older double-hung windows with many wooden components can jam as the wood warps.

Maintenance of double-hung windows means you need to check the lift strings of the windows. If you notice in the track of the lower window panel of a double-hung window, you will notice a string or cable. Some of the older and larger double-hung windows will also have a small chain in the track. Inside the shaft, there is a weight which can help hold the window in the open position.

Proper maintenance is simply make sure that none of the finish is pealing off. If you notice that paint or finish is pealing off the windows and the wood is starting to grey, then it's time to sand the windows down and give a good finish.

Making double-hung windows is very complicated and we don't recommend doing this yourselves. This takes a special kind of workmanship. If you like double-hung windows, we recommend going to a home improvement warehouse and order a high quality brand, such as Pella or Andersen.

Alternatives to Double-Hung Windows
If you want to be unique and have your own window construction, we do have some alternatives to double-hung windows.

The basic hinged window is probably the easiest to build yourself. Think of it as being a set of cabinet doors, but more heavy duty. Simply take a couple of 2X4s of a high quality wood and make the basic structure of the window frame. You should make the windows double pain for added insulation. This can easily be done by using a router with a fine router bit and carve a groove and a half groove in the 2X4s and then using a miter saw, cut 45 degree angles in the sides of the 2X4s. Then take some 1X2s and cut them to the size of the 2X4s. Make sure the glass fits snugly into the grooves and install the first outer pain after the three of the four parts of the frame have been assembled as shown below in Figure Twelve.

Figure

Twelve: The basic window

Figure 12a   Figure 12b

Notice in Figure 12a, the 2X4s are assembled and the first pain is inserted. Then as shown in Figure 12b, the first pain is installed and the top 2X4 is affixed to the other three. Now, the second pain is placed and the 1X2s are put in and fastened with wood adhesive and finish nails. The side of the 1X2s should be the inside window. You then want to place a lip on both windows to keep heat or cooling from escaping outside. You also want to get special insulation tape which you can get at any home improvement store and tape it to the hinged side of the windows. Get some V tape which is a plastic tape which folds out into a V and one side of the V has adhesive. This is for the top and the bottom of the window. This gives a good seal. Tape the V tape should have the point facing inside for easy opening and closing.

Making a Russian fortochka is a neat feature you can incorporate into your window construction. A fortochka is a small window which can be opened in the wintertime to air out rooms. Simply follow the steps above and make one of the panels lower than the other and add an extra frame and follow the steps of a hinged window on a smaller scale. Note, the fortochka is usually on one side of the window, so you don't need to make a lip on it.

The Best Woods to Use
When making windows and doors which are a barrier from your inside to the great outdoors, you want to keep in mind that harder woods are better. Pine is good, but you will want to get the higher quality varieties of pine, such as aspen, cedar, or redwood when using any of the evergreen woods. The regular pine used for 2X4s is not the greatest wood for the elements. Other good woods include oak, walnut, and teak. Teak is fairly expensive, and can be hard to get. Teak is one of the hardest woods in the world and is often used in boat building.

Windows and doors are a necessity and can be some of the most challenging woodworking projects. Maintenance of these can also be difficult as the doors and windows facing the outside often see the elements. If a building or home you own has been abandoned for a long time and not been cared for, then you can run into rot and other problems. Hence we've included this chapter.

Chapter Eight

Boat Building

A fun project which you can do with your children, especially if you live on a large lake, river, or on the seaside. Boat building can involve a wide variety of different projects. You can create canoes, scows, skiffs, or bunts. You can build rowboats, sailboats, and more. In this chapter, you will learn all the following maritime projects.

A. **Building a scow** is one of the most simple boat building projects and is ideal to get started with. A scow is more like a barge than a boat. Typically, scows are used as rowboats in areas where the water is not turbulent. Ideal bodies of water for scows are rivers, small ponds and lakes, and large swamps. Scows make ideal fishing boats in those types of water bodies.
B. **Building a bunt** is a bit more challenging than building a scow, but you can use a bunt as both a rowboat or a sail boat. Bunt boats have a bow which is smaller than the aft transom but is still not pointed, like a skiff. Bunts can be used in choppier waters, such as large lakes and bay areas of seas and oceans.
C. **Building your skiff** and outfitting it as a sailboat: A skiff is ideal for all kinds of bodies of water. The skiff can be made into a small cat rigged or sloop rigged sailboat for day excursions on large lakes or oceans. The skiff is designed to land on a beach and can be used as both a rowboat or sailboat.
D. **Building a sailboat** using either a skiff or bunt model. By following the above instructions on building a bunt or skiff, you will learn how to build a dagger board and insert for dagger board in the boat. You will also learn why you need a dagger board for a sailboat. You will also learn how to make a tiller operated rudder and how to outfit your boat with a removable mast for either a cat, sloop, or lateen rigging. You will also learn what kinds of fabrics are ideal for sails.

Introduction to Basic Boat Building
Before we get into the projects mentioned above, we want to cover the basics of boat building and why it is so complicated, if not one of the most complicated woodworking undertakings to get involved in.

Water and wood can be a serious problem if the correct finishes are used. This is especially true when it comes to wooden boats. Basically, water is the worst enemy of wood. Add salt water to the equation, then you can have serious damage to wood. This is why there is a need for special marine glues and finishes to coat the wood which comes into contact with the surrounding water.

Curved shapes are also very difficult to form with boats. This poses the biggest challenges, especially when building a skiff design around the bow, but not so much so with a bunt construction. It takes special equipment to bend wood without breaking it. You have learned how to do this in some of the previous chapters, but when it comes to boat building, this has to be done on a large scale.

Dagger boards and keels are important for sailboats. This can also provide a challenge in construction. Basically, sailboats are top heavy with their masts. When a sailboat sails against the wind, it has to tack and move in a zigzag motion. When sailboats move is such a motion, they will lean over to one side. If the keel or dagger board is not present, there is no counter weight to offset the mast and your sailboat will capsize.

Acquiring marine hardware when building boats, especially for sailboats and larger boats are not found at your local hardware or home improvement store. There is also no marine department at any of the bigger home improvement chains, such as Menard's, Lowe's, or Home Depot. So what do you do about that? Well, if you live on the seaside or near a large body of water where boating is popular, chances are that there is a marina where you can get boat building supplies, such as hardware and special marine finishes.

Motors and wooden boats can also require a special skill. You will need to know how to strengthen your boat's transom to be able to support an outboard motor. When building house boats, which are bulky and function more as barges, you will have to learn how to manage two outboard motors if you do not want to keep your houseboat permanently moored in some marina.

Maintenance of wooden boats can also be very labor intensive, thus you will need to learn how to properly care for and repair damage from exposure to extreme elements in a maritime environment. Likewise, when having a yacht, most areas in the world do have strict hygiene and health regulations for toilets, thus you can no longer have a toilet or a system which simply dumps your waste, including excrement into the water. You can get special septic systems for boats which can break down waste and excrement with either chemical or biological systems. This is also something to take into account when undertaking such large boats, on which you would like spend the night on.

The best woods for boat building should be hard woods which can handle high humidity and are less likely to rot. Typically, the ideal wood for boat building is teak and teak was used by many of the ship builders who built the old square rigged tall ships, such as the clipper ships and the windjammers. Teak is a difficult wood to find, so oak would be the next best option.

Building a Scow
One of the simplest boats to build is a scow. What exactly is a scow? A scow is a rowboat which is built in the typical barge construction.

What makes a scow so simple to build is that there is no wood to bend or shape. The one disadvantage of a scow is that it is not a boat for choppy waters. If you live on a small pond or lake or a river. Typically, people who live along the seaside or a large lake with high waves, like the Great Lakes would prefer a bunt or a skiff, which has more of a point and is able to cut through the chop easier. We'll get to those later.

Building a scow skeleton can very simply be done. When building the skeleton of the scow, simply take oak 2X6s to form a barge like structure as shown in Figure One below. For ribs, you can use oak 2X4s.

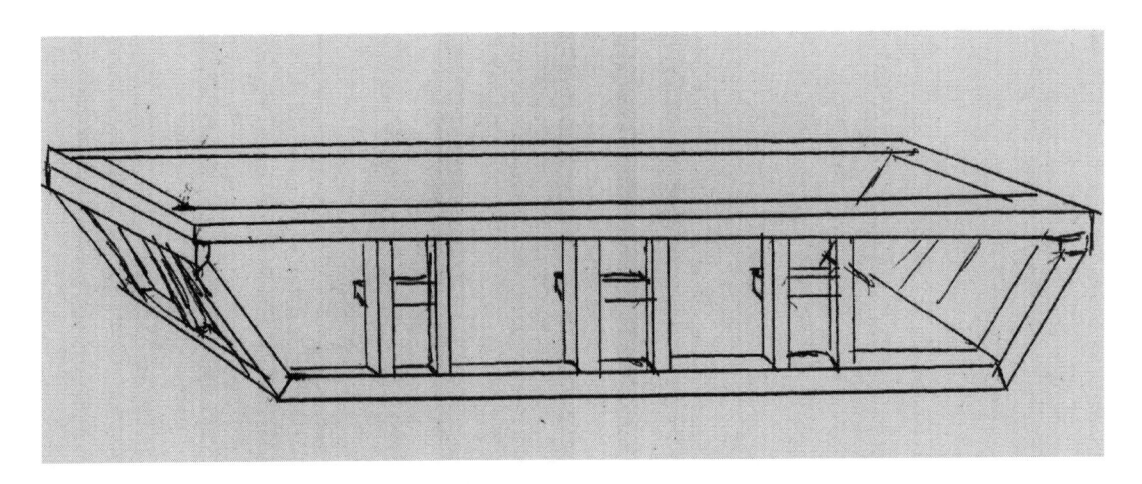

Figure One: Basic skeletal construction of a scow

Notice that the skeleton of the scow which is being built in Figure One above is a classic flat bottom. Flat bottoms are ideal for rivers, ponds, or small lakes where there is no chop. Choppy waters are not ideal for flat bottoms, as waves can get under the bottom of a flat bottomed boat and capsize it.

You need to use a special marine plywood or oak planks to make the planking which covers the skeletal structure of the scow. You can use oak 2X12s for seats in the scow.

Scows are mostly used as row boats or pedal boats. Though we will not show you how to make a pedal boat here, as the mechanism is quite complicated, they do work similarly to the pedal system of a bicycle. In this chapter, however, we will cover more the items you will need for a scow as a rowboat.

Oarlocks are needed for a rowboat. Oarlocks can be bought at any boating hardware store which sells the hardware needed for wooden boats. An oarlock holds the oars in place and allows for free movement for effective rowing. You can also apply this for building a bunt or skiff to use as a rowboat.

Making the oars is not as difficult as it seems. To make the oars, you will need the following tools.

A. **A jigsaw** to cut the tapered areas around the paddles and the handle as well as the rounded corners of the bottom of the paddles.
B. **A table saw** to cut the 2X12 to size at the handle.
C. **A lave** to round out the handles of the oars and allow for rotation in the oarlocks.
D. **A power plane** to plane the shape of the oars into the proper thickness.
E. **A power sander** to sand the oars and paddles of the oars in the proper curvature for good propulsion of the scow through the water.

When making the oars, you want to first draw the initial shape of the oar on the 2X12 and then cut the areas shown in red with a jigsaw as shown in Figure Two below. The lines in black can be cut with a table saw. When using the table saw, use care not to cut into the paddle area. Use the jigsaw to cut enough into the straight line to avoid the circular blade of the table saw cutting into the paddle.

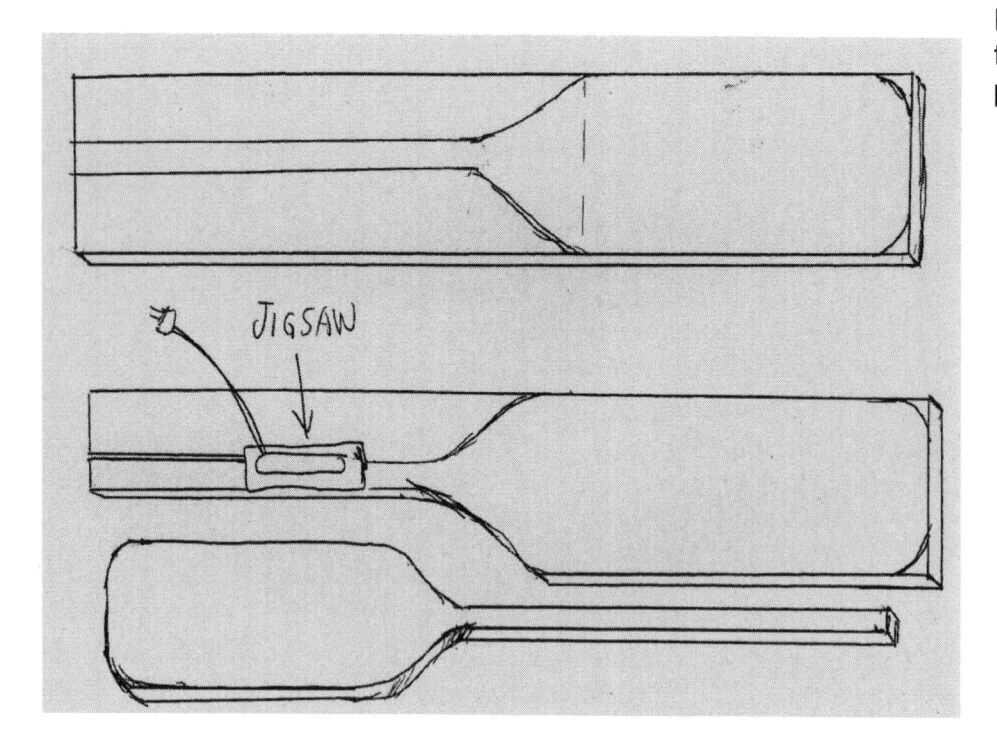

Figure Two: Cutting the shape of the paddle into the 2X12.

Notice that the 2X12 is initially too thick for the paddle, but just right for the handle, thus the need for the lave and the power plane.

The handle of the oar needs to be rounded, thus you need to learn how to skillfully use a lave before you can do this project. Place the paddle into the lave by locking the paddle end of the oar to the far end of the lave which can have an adjustable vice to clamp it into place. Take the flat knife which comes with the lave and cut into the handle part of the oar until it is completely round. Do not carve into the paddle, as that can be shaped with a power plane and sander.

After you finished the rounding of the handle of the oar, you will notice that the top of the paddle is more square and still has more of the shape of the 2X12, as shown in Figure Three below.

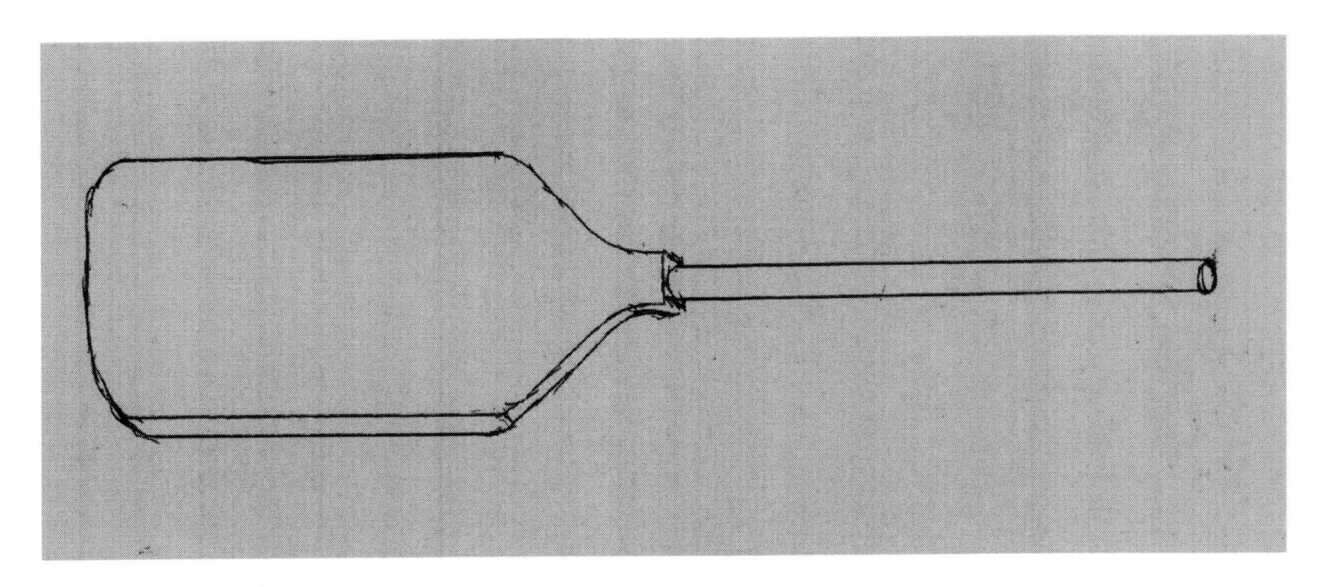

Figure Three: The look of the oar once the handle has been rounded

Notice that in Figure Three above, the handle has been basically completed. You want to have the handle of the oar to be as round as a dowel rod. There is a reason why the oar's handle needs to be round. A round handle allows for free movement within the oarlock and allows you to have the paddle in a vertical position when in the water for maximum propulsion and horizontal while in the air to allow quick movement of the vessel.

Shaping the paddle needs to be done with a couple of tools. With the use of a power hand plane, you can smooth the corners of the paddle and make it flow with the rounded handle which was just carved in the lave. Then take the power plane to plane each side of the paddle in order to taper the two broad flat sides of the paddle until they have a flat but pointed bottom of the paddle. Then use the power sander to smooth out all the edges and have a nice flowing shape to have an oar which is both aero and aqua dynamic for effective propulsion of your scow. You need to make the oars the same way if you plan to build a bunt or skiff as a rowboat as well.   See Figure Four below to see how the finished oar should look like.

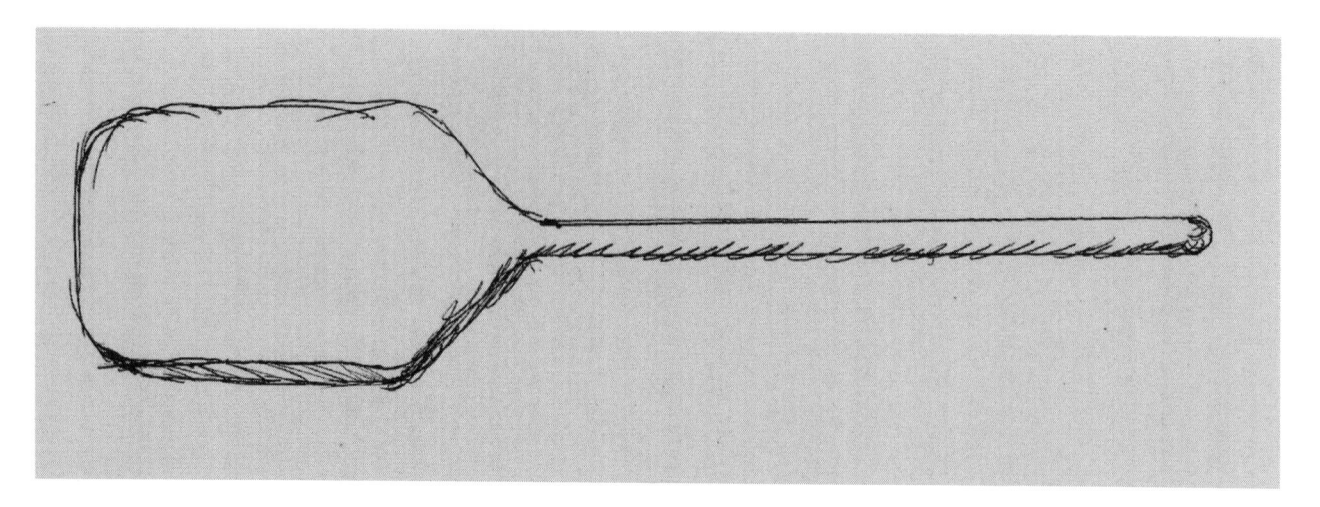

Figure Four: The finished oar ready for a good marine finish

Skinning the scow basically means adding the planking and turning the skeleton into an actual boat. If you use marine plywood, the job is fairly easy. Use a good heavy duty marine glue and calk to seal all the seams and prevent the scow from taking on water. Use heavy duty boat screws to fasten the planking to the skeletal ribs of the scow and then use a spar urethane marine finish or marine paint to finish the vessel. Note, when adding seats, screw in the 2X12s using the same marine glue and calk before you apply the final finish. Position the seats in such a way that they will not interfere with the rowing motions in the boat.

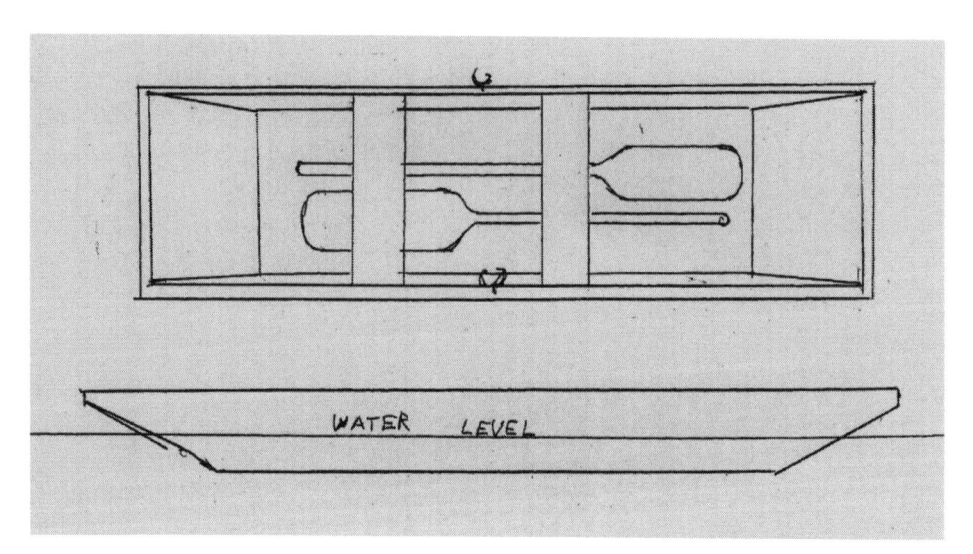

Figure Five: The finished scow

A scow can be a great boat for those of you who live on the edge of a large pond or lake, or even along a large, wide, and deep river with a mild current. Recreational uses for a scow can range from enjoying a good row around the pond, lake, or river, fishing, or other waterside activities. You can also modify a scow to add a small electric trawling outboard motor for the avid freshwater fishing.

Building a Bunt
What is a bunt? Well, basically, a bunt is a type of a boat which is similar to a scow. It has either a flat bottom, like a scow or can also have a shallow V-bottom. A bunt is a little bit more difficult type of a boat to build than a scow as there is some wood bending involved in building a bunt.

Building the skeleton of the bunt is more involved than the scow which was covered above. When building a bunt, you will notice that the bow is still square, similar to a scow, but unlike the scow, the boat's front transom is not as slanted outward as the scow, but at the same time, it still goes a little bit more outward. The nice thing about the bunt is that you can have a V bottom versus a flat bottom so it will be able to handle more chop than a scow. See Figure Six below to see the beginning of the construction of the skeleton of a bunt.

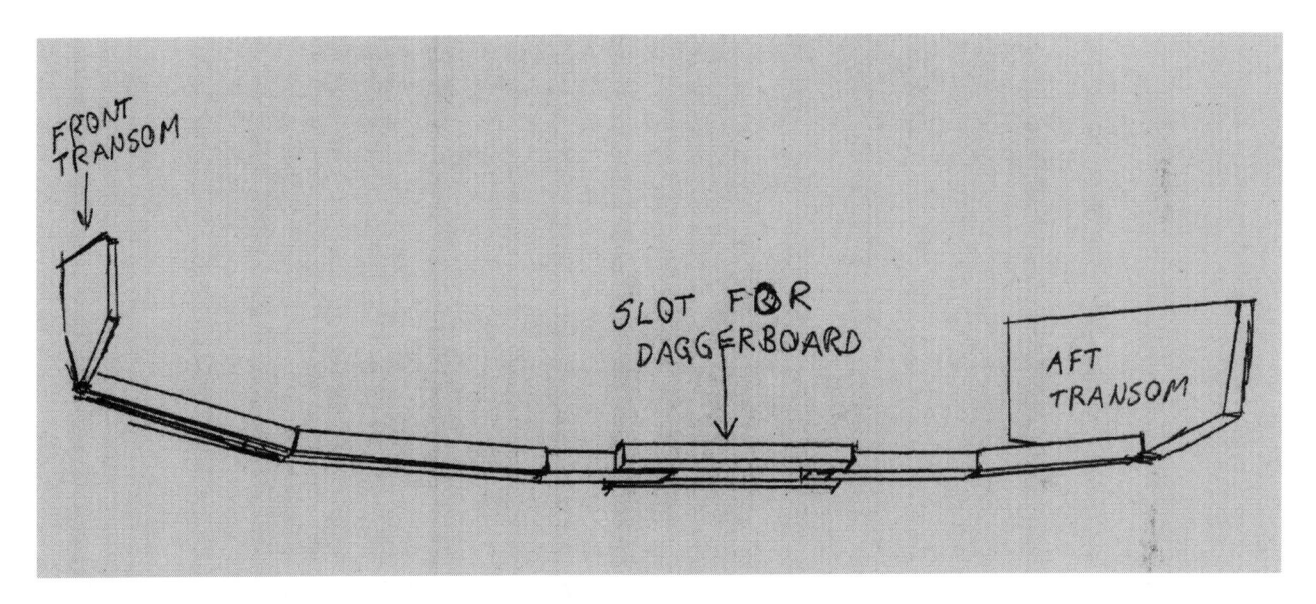

Figure Six: The basic skeleton of the bunt construction before adding the ribs
Figure Six above shows the basic beginning of building the skeleton of the bunt. You start with the keelson, which is the main beam which goes from the bow to the aft. You then add the bunt plate and the rear transom. Notice that the keelson is also slightly bent and the bunt is slightly higher than the rear transom. Basically, when making the keelson, you will have to use several pieces of wood to make the keelson. The keelson will be too thick to bend one solid piece of wood.

Depending on the size of the bunt you are building, you will need a fairly strong keelson, because it is the backbone of the entire boat. If your boat is between six to ten feet, which is a good size for a bunt that you want to keep at the beach, we recommend you use 2X6s or 2X8s to make the keelson. In many cases, if you want to make a sailboat, you will have to modify the keelson to have a slot for a dagger board, which you will learn how to make later. See Figure Seven below on how to fashion the keelson for a bunt.

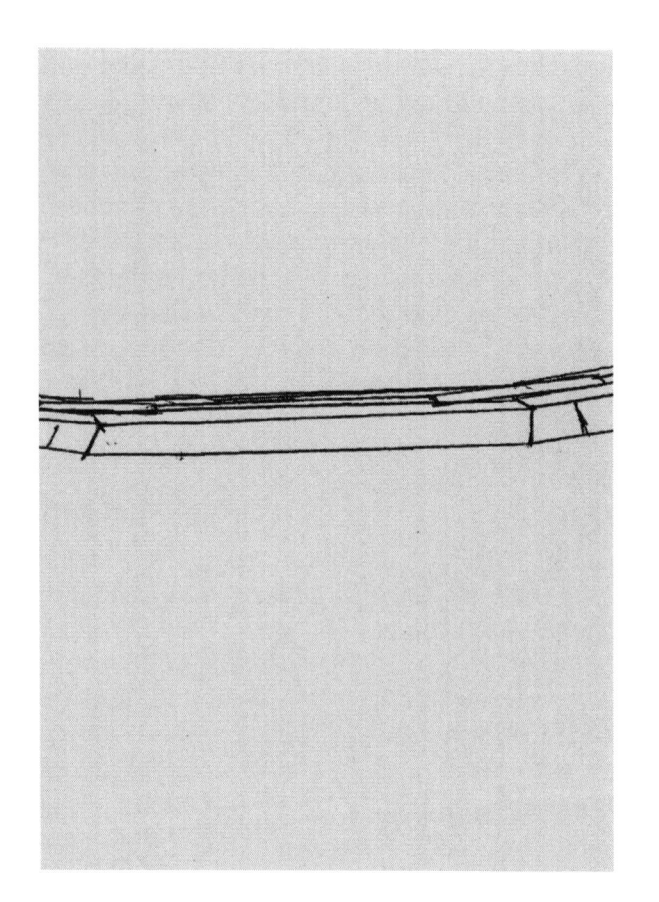

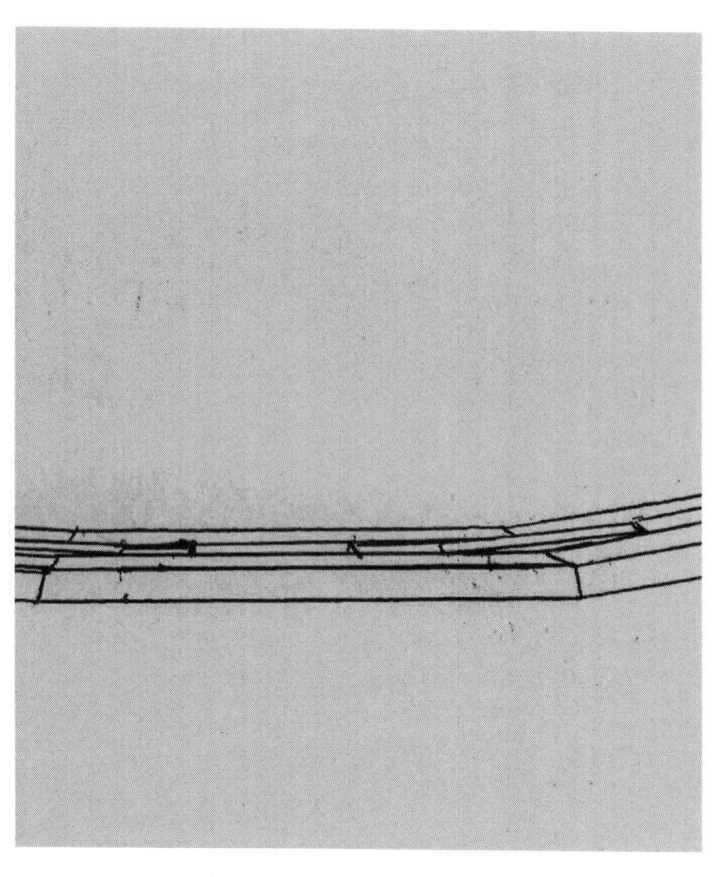

Figure Seven: The keelson for a bunt as a rowboat and as a sailboat
Figure 7a   Figure 7b

Notice in Figure 7a, the keelson is made for a bunt which is to be a simple rowboat. Figure 7b, on the other hand shows how the keelson needs to be built for a small sailboat. Notice the circled area, this is the slot for the dagger board. Eventually, you will also have to build a stack to surround the dagger board to prevent water from coming into the boat.

Building the ribs for your bunt is much simpler than building the keelson. The keelson is the major part of your bunt's skeletal structure, but you also need the ribs to hold the planking which in turn makes the boat. Like fashioning the keelson, the ribs are also too thick to bend, so you have to construct them in a similar fashion as you did with the keelson.

Symmetry is critical when it comes to building the ribs, as anything that is slightly asymmetrical can cause instability in the water. This can be especially dangerous if you are planning to build a sailboat. If the hull is asymmetrical, when you tack, the boat can capsize.

To make the ribs symmetrical is rather simple. Cut everything into the proper angles and cut the same size for both sides. In other words, when you make one side, use the pieces as templates of each other and then you turn the ones for the opposite side over and your ribs will be symmetrical. You want to build the ribs with the small ones first then the larger ones. Start by building by the bunt at the very bow first and at the aft transom in the back and meet them in the middle. The ribs should be at least a foot apart from each other in a ten foot sailboat. If the boat is bigger, the ribs should be closer together for extra strength. Add temporary struts to hold the ribs straight until you can get the rims put on. See Figures Eight and Nine on proper rib construction.

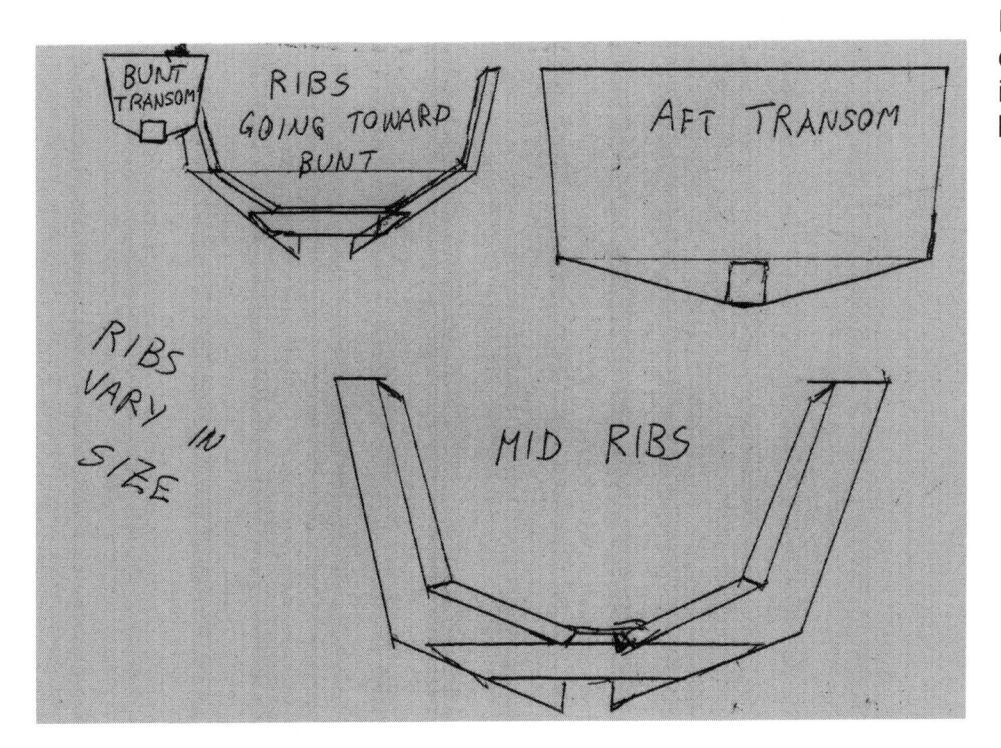

Figure Eight: Basic construction for the individual ribs from bunt to transom

Notice that at the bottom of the ribs there is a notch. This notch allows the entire rib to be easily affixed to the keelson. Each rib should be bolted to the keelson with at least three bolts all the way through for a strong fit. You want to make sure that the ribs are plum when they are installed.

Figure Nine: Ribs fastened to the keelson and the skeletal structure is already beginning to look like a boat.

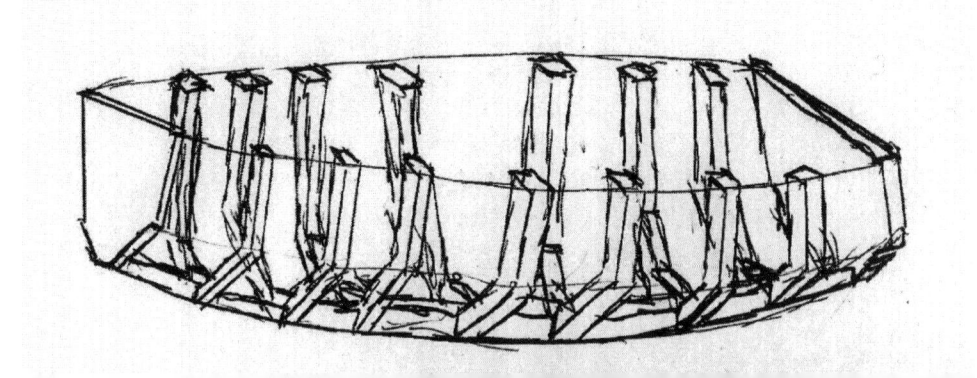

Now that you have the ribs in place and temporary struts to ensure the ribs remain plum, you are ready to make the rims which get fastened to the top of the boat.

The rims are about as thick as the ribs, so it is no use in bending them. Ideally, when building a rim, you want to take a 2X6 and miter them to the curvature of the boat. Make a second layer and put them together as you would lay bricks. This makes for a strong rim and a sturdy boat construction. See Figure Ten below.

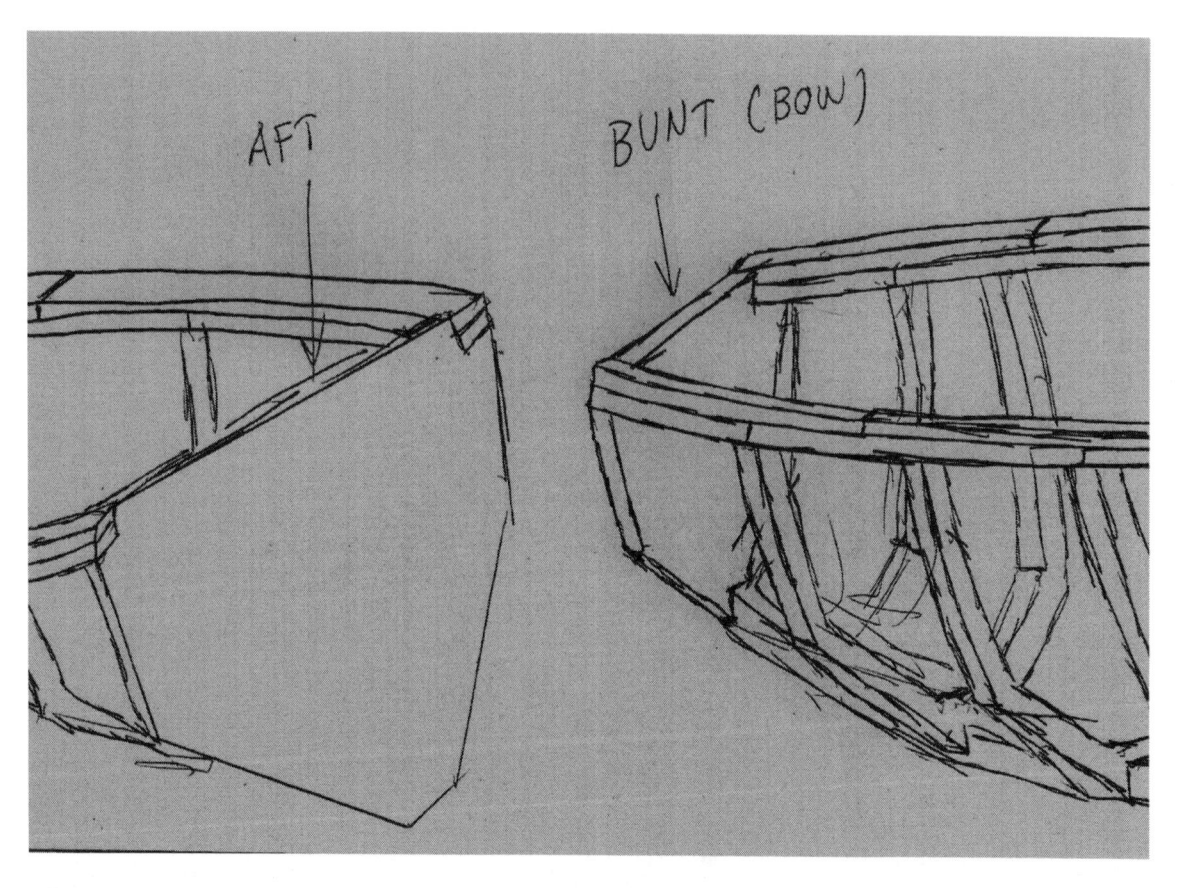

Figure Ten: The rims which strengthen the bunt's skeletal structure.
Notice that Figure Ten shows how the rim is several pieces of wood which are screwed onto the top of the ribs and the pieces are placed together like bricks, to give extra strength. You want to

use your miter saw to cut some of the rim pieces at a slight angle. Then, when you have the two layers of 2X6s or 2X8s, depending on the size of your boat, then simply take a corse sander to sand the rough corners of the rim boards to smooth the rim.

Adding the planking to your bunt finalizes the job and your boat will then be ready for a good marine finish. When getting the wood for planking, you can either get marine plywood sheets or special planks of solid wood from a special lumberyard which has a specialty department for woods used in boat building.

Bending planks to shape is a slow and tedious process. You will want to fashion a special steamer which will steam the wood for a long time. Steaming the wood adds moisture to it, making the fibers pliable. This will keep it from cracking or splintering on you as you fasten it to the skeletal structure of the boat. See Figures Eleven and Twelve below to see how to steam the wood and fasten it to the bunt's basic skeletal structure.

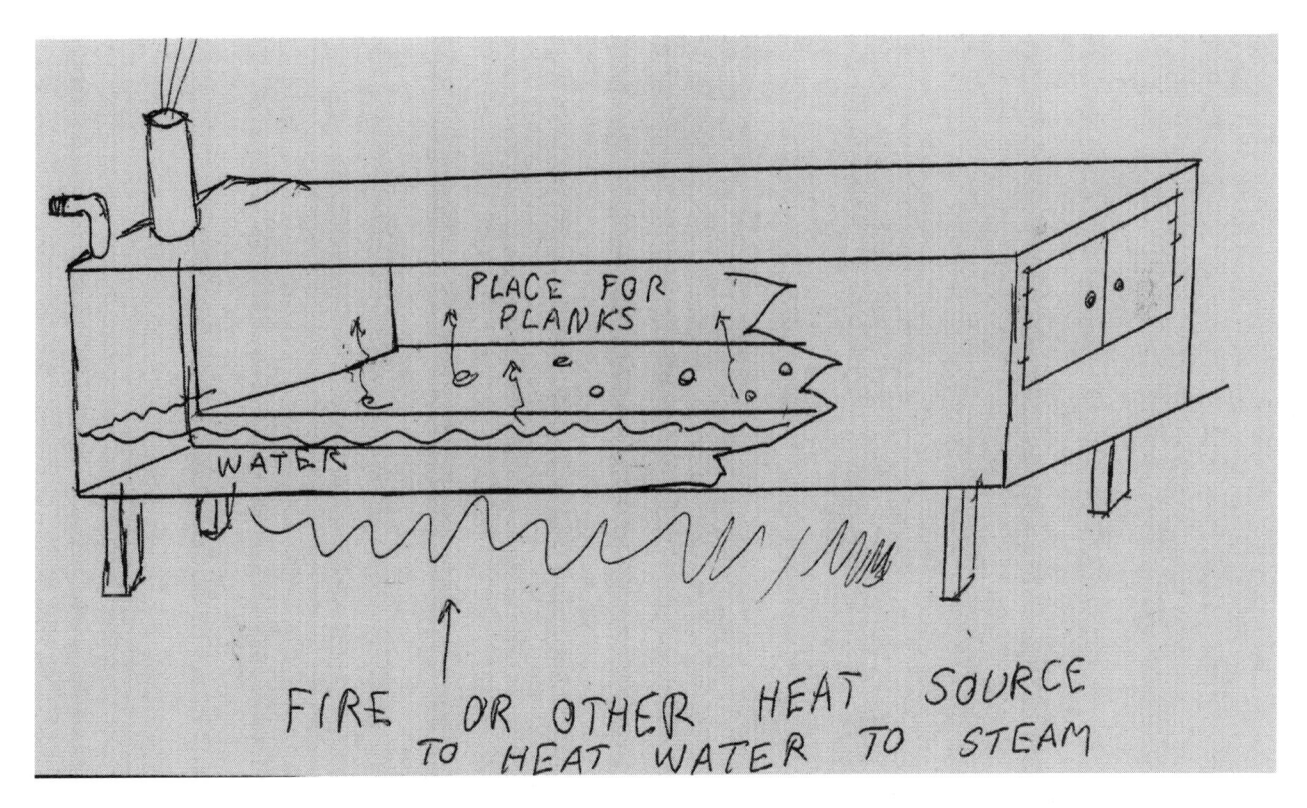

Figure Eleven: Wood steamer for boat planks.
Notice that the wood is on a couple of blocks and you have a large vat of water which you get hot enough to boil. The steam flow is controlled and goes through the area where the wood is. Wood planking should be steamed for at least four hours before it can be pliable enough to shape and bend.

When screwing on the planking, you want to make sure that the marine calking is being used to keep the seams and areas where the screws are from being leaky. NEVER nail the planking. Always use screws when building any kind of boat, whether a scow, bunt, or skiff. Nails might pop out as the wood expands and contracts.

Building a Skiff

When building a skiff, you can expect to have more challenges than building a bunt. Unlike a bunt, which has some bending involved in its construction, a skiff has a pointed bow, thus you need to make the planking pliable enough to bend to the point of the bow.

Typically, if you want to build a rowboat or sailboat which can handle rough chop, the skiff construction is the best way to go. The reason why a skiff is good for rough chop is because of its pointed bow. The pointed bow allows for it to cut through the waves you would find in oceanic waters or the waters of large lakes, such as the Great Lakes.

More bottom options come with building a skiff. Unlike a scow, which only has a flat bottom, or a bunt which typically has a flat or shallow V-bottom, a skiff can have either a shallow or deep V-bottom. The type of bottom a boat has is also important to what kind of chop it can handle. The deeper the V-bottom, the less likely it is for waves to be able to curl under the bottom of the boat and capsize it.

Building a skiff is much like building a bunt. You first start with the skeleton of the boat. The skeleton is always the most important structure as it is what holds the entire boat together.

Building the skiff is a bit different from building a bunt. Unlike the bunt construction, as skiff only has one transom, in the aft of the boat, that is the rear. Like with the bunt, you want to start building the skiff with the keelson. The keelson is the strongest part of the skeleton and holds the entire rib structure together.

Like when building a bunt, the keelson of a skiff is too thick to be bent, thus you will need to fashion it together with three layers of 2X8s to 2X12s, depending on how large a vessel you want to build. Typically, if you are planning to build a boat which is about six to eight feet long, 2X8s are sufficient for the keelson. See Figure Twelve below to see how the keelson of a skiff needs to be built.

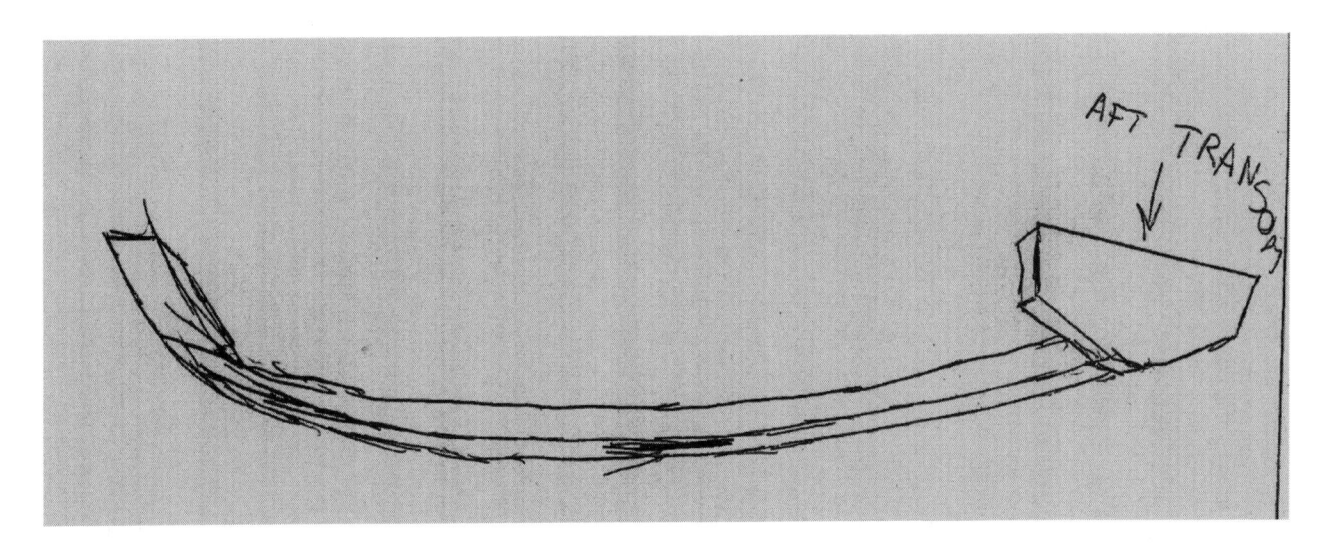

Figure Twelve: The keelson of a skiff

Notice how the bow is merely the extension of the keelson and allows you to direct the shape of the V for the bottom. In Figure Twelve above, the design is for a deep V-bottom skiff. Notice that with the bow strut of the skiff skeleton, the wood is a bit thicker. For example, if you are using 2X8s to make the keelson, you want to use a 2X12 for the bow strut. This needs to be strong, so it can support smaller ribs to strengthen the bow. Furthermore, when building a larger vessel, like a yacht, you may want to have a bow sprit if you have a sloop, yawl, ketch, or schooner. The bow strut has to be strong enough to support that.

Building the ribs of a skiff is very similar to building the ribs of a bunt. The concept of using 2X6s for a six to eight foot boat are the same, but with the depth of the V-bottom, the angles can change. The difference lies when constructing the skiff is with the ribs near the bow. The bow of a skiff does not have a transom, like the bunt does. This means that the keelson of a skiff basically goes up the bow to the very deck of the boat, if there is one. Usually, the smaller skiffs are open without a deck, thus in that case, the keelson goes up to above the rim. See Figure Thirteen below about how the individual ribs of a skiff are assembled.

Figure Thirteen: The ribs of a skiff

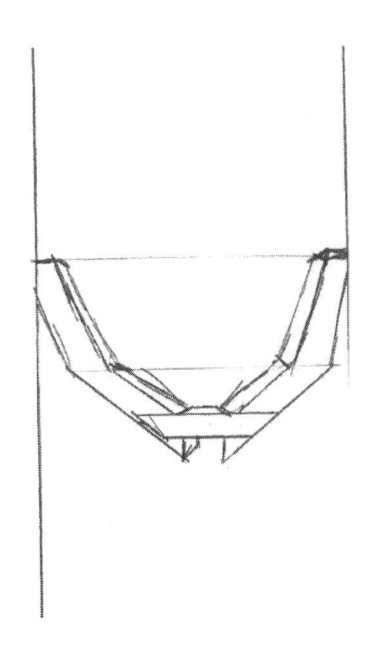

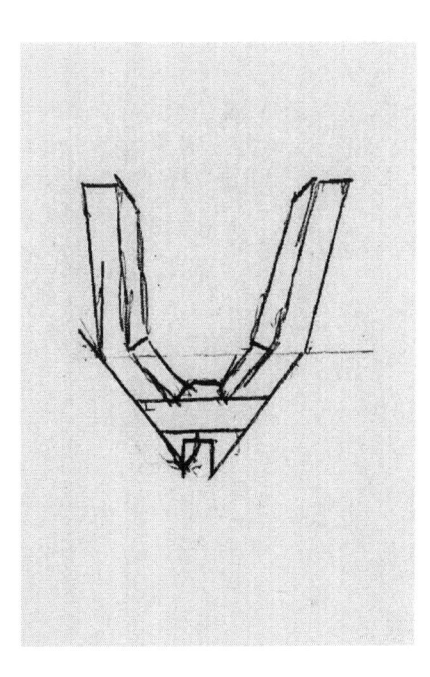

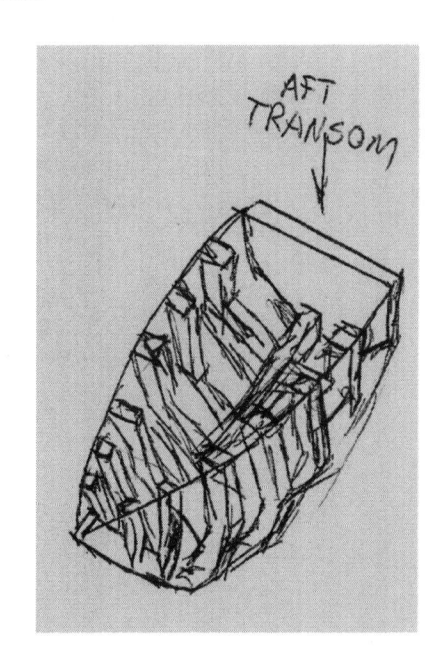

Figure 13a   Figure 13b   Figure 13c

Notice that in Figure 13a, the ribs are those for the main part of the hull. These ribs are built similarly to those of a bunt, but this skiff has a deep V-bottom, so the ribs have more of a V shape to them. Figure 13b shows the smaller ribs for the bow of the skiff. Figure 13c shows how the whole skeletal structure is fitted together.

Building the rim of the skiff is similar to building the rim of a bunt. You want to use different pieces of 2X6s or 2X8s, depending on the size of your boat and make two or three rows in a brick fashion. The whole purpose of the rim is to strengthen the ribs of the boat. Once the rim is completed, you can then add the planking.

Adding the planking on a skiff requires more bending than a bunt, so you want to follow the same directions you read above for building a bunt, but when it comes to making a skiff, you will have to bend more, so the planks should be steamed until they are completely pliable.

Building a Sailboat
Now that you have learned how to build both a bunt and a skiff, you can easily convert them into a sailboat by following the projects below. Basically, building a sailboat entails several projects in itself. You will need to learn how to build the mast and rigging, and also to keep the mast secure in the boat. You will also have to learn how to build a daggerboard, a rudder, and you will also have to learn the right knots to keep the sails secure in the wind.

Building the daggerboard is one of the simplest projects of building a sailboat. Basically, a daggerboard is a removable keel and is ideal for sailboats you like to keep in shallow waters and land on the beach.

Typically, the daggerboard is a 2X12 which can have some lead weights imbedded in the bottom. Typically, a 2X12 is wide enough to be a daggerboard for most sailboats which are no longer than ten to 15 feet. If you want to build a bigger sailboat, you will have to build a fixed keel. This will be covered in more detail below.

When making the keel part of the daggerboard, you will want to round the corners of the 2X12 to make it more aqua-dynamic. You will also want to bevel the sides and bottom of the 2X12 on both sides. You then want to take a 2X6 or 2X8 to place at the top of the 2X12 and affix it so it looks like a dagger, hence the name. When complete with its construction, you will want to add some lead weights in the bottom of the daggerboard. See Figure Fourteen below to see how the completed daggerboard should look like.

Figure Fourteen: The typical daggerboard

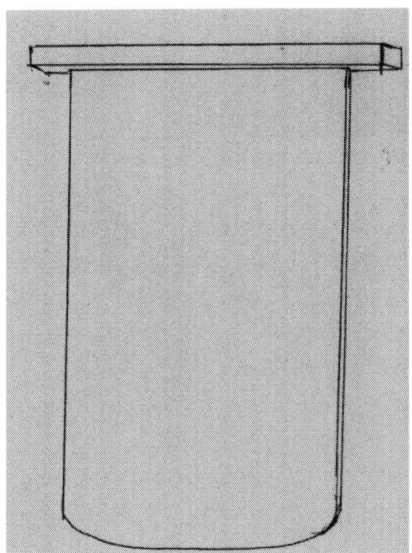

Notice that in Figure Fourteen above, the daggerboard has a hole with some putty in it. This is special marine putty and it holds some lead weights in the bottom of the daggerboard. The lead weights are there to help keep the sailboat stable in deep water and minimize the risk of capsizing.

The mast and rigging on a sailboat are just as important as the daggerboard. The mast and rigging is the backbone of the sail, which is your primary unit of propulsion of a sailboat.

When it comes to the mast and the rigging, there are three types of components you need to remember. These things also differ from the type of rigging you plan to build. Different types of riggings for a small sailboat set up as a skiff or bunt are listed below.

A. **Cat rigging** is the simplest rigging to build. The cat rigging consists of a mast, boom, and one sail, the main sail. The main sail is a right triangle with the 90 degree corner at the area where the boom is fastened to the mast.
B. **Sloop rigging** is a bit more complicated, but not too difficult to construct. A sloop consists of two sails, a main sail which is fastened to the mast and the boom, just like in a cat rigging, but also has a second sail in front, a jib. The jib is not adjusted as much as the main sail, but it does aid in wind propulsion of the sailboat. In fact, a sloop can move much faster than a cat rigging, as it has that extra sail for the wind to propel the boat along.
C. **Gaff riggings** are typically used in larger sailboats, such as schooners, which you will learn how to build later, but if you like the old-fashioned look, you can create a gaff rigging. Gaff riggings have a main boom, but also at the top of the mast, they have an auxiliary boom which is pointed upward at an angle. This is a complex rigging to build and will be reserved for the segment on seafaring sailboats.
D. **Lateen rigging** is the type of rigging which is also somewhat complicated to build. The lateen rigging consists of a shorter mast and two booms which join each other at a point towards the bow of the sailboat. The sail is placed between the two booms and the booms are fastened to the side of the mast with circular rings.

Before we go on with rigging construction, we need to discuss what would be the best materials for sails. Back in the old days, sails were made from heavy duty hemp canvas, however, canvas has a tendency to mildew and rot. Today, we have a wide variety of heavy duty nylon fabrics which are made specifically for sails, hang gliders, parachutes, and ultra-light aircraft. You also have kevlar which is just as heavy duty if not stronger than nylon. These are the ideal materials for sails. You may want to have your sails professionally tailored by someone who is expert in making sails for sailboats.

The cat rigging is your most basic of riggings. If you have a bunt, this is the best kind of rigging. Because a bunt has a more square bow, it will not be able to go as fast through the waves as a skiff, so there is no need for a jib. Skiffs, on the other hand, can be outfitted with either a cat or sloop rigging.

When building the mast and boom for your cat rigging, you will want to take a 4X4 and carve it round in your lave. The mast and boom have to be perfectly round and you can do this by getting a special knife for your lave which has a flat blade, shaped like a spade. You may also want to set up a special jig which is set up for a fixed position. You can move this jig back and forth along a track to ensure even cutting of the post. Adjust the incursion of the knife little by little and have it carve into the wood until you hear no more grinding, then move it to the next section until the 4X4 post is completely round. Do the same thing with the boom, but when you are finished carving the mast round, carve a groove at the base of the mast, where the boom is to go. You will then want to get some thin cable and fit it with some ballbearings which are strung along the cable. The cable needs to be tightly fastened to the mast and prevented from moving up or down.

You will want to carve a hole in the top of the mast and attach a pulley for the lanyard. The lanyard is the rope which hoists the sail up and down. For a cat rigging, you will need one hole and one pulley, but for a sloop you will need two, one for the main sail and one for the jib.

Towards the middle of the boat, you will need to install a boom track. This is part of the rigging which has a car with a set of pulleys on it. This allows you to control the movement of the boom while sailing. This is very important, especially during tacking. Tacking is how you maneuver the boom and the main sail when sailing upwind. During tacking, the boom can swing from side to side with great force and this can be deadly for anyone who gets hit in the head with the boom. The boom track and pulleys are a mechanism to keep the boom from coming completely loose, as you will need to maintain the sail at a certain angle when going upwind. You want to make sure the boom is high enough to pass overhead or to allow room for easy ducking.

You can also control the rope as it goes through the pulleys on the boom track, letting more rope out when sailing down wind and less rope when sailing upwind. See Figure Fifteen below for a typical cat rigging.

Figure Fifteen: The typical cat rigging

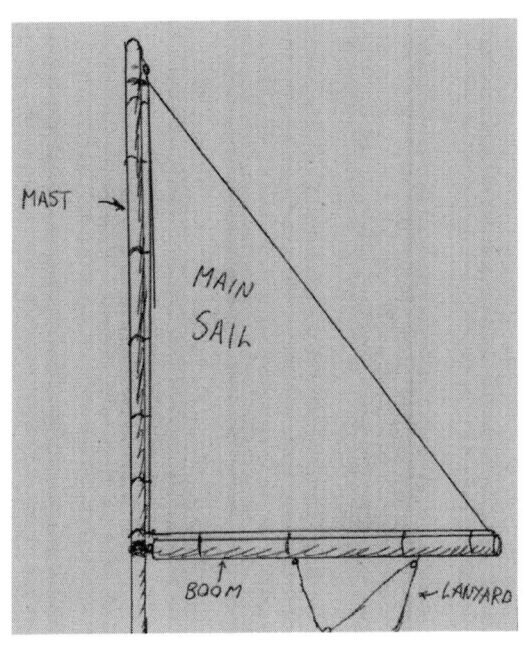

Notice in Figure Fifteen above, the cat rigging has the single main sail and the boom with the boom track in the boat. Note that when sailing, you want to keep inexperienced people, especially children away from the boom track, as the boom can shift violently when the wind shifts and during tacking.

Building the rudder and tiller is the next project you need to learn when making a sailboat. The rudder and tiller, also known as the governor, is key in directing the boat and in which way you want the sailboat to turn. The rudder is a large paddle which is attached to special hinges on the transom in the back of the boat and the tiller is the handle which you hold to govern the rudder. When the rudder is straight, the boat goes straight, when you pivot the rudder, the boat can turn right or left depending on which direction you turn the rudder. A sailboat relies both on the water, with the rudder, and on the wind, with the main sail to turn. The main sail is especially important when tacking upwind, but the rudder also plays an important role.

When making the rudder, you want to take a piece of 2X12 which is about three to four feet long and cut it into a paddle shape. The wide part of the paddle needs to be at the bottom and the narrow part needs to be up at the top with at least six inches above the aft transom for easy movement. One side of the rudder needs to be straight and the other side curved. The straight side needs to be facing the transom. You can get special rudder hinges at any marina which sells wooden boat hardware. The pins are affixed to a special bracket which is screwed to the rudder itself. The holes for the pins are then screwed on the transom. The pins of the rudder hinges have points on the bottom to facilitate placing and removing the rudder. Like the daggerboard, the rudder may also need to be removed when idling in shallow waters.

Once you have cut the rudder in shape, you will want to bevel all edges except the straight edge which gets fastened to the transom with the hinges. See Figure Sixteen below to see how the rudder is made and fastened to the transom.

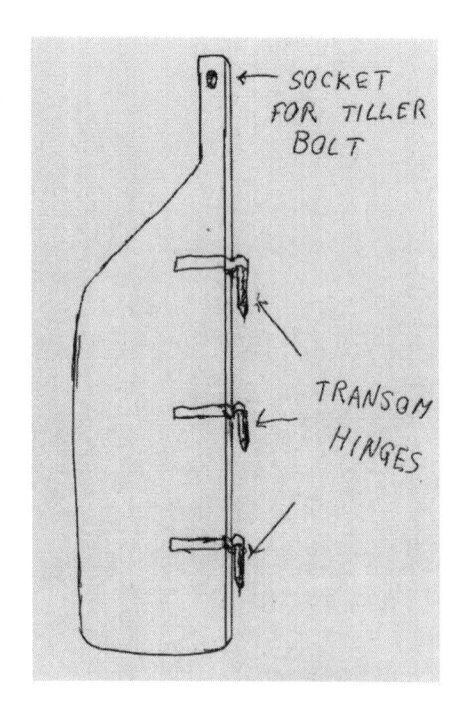

Figure Sixteen: The basic rudder without the tiller

You can see how the rudder can easily be placed or removed into the hinges on the transom. Now, you need to build the tiller and attach it to the rudder. Basically, the tiller needs to pivot up and down so you can fold it next to the rudder for easy storage in the boat when not in use. This is simply done by taking a couple of 2X4s in about eight inches in length and bolt them to the top of the rudder. Then you want to take a 2X2 from anywhere of a foot to a foot and a half in length for the tiller. Drill a hole in the tiller and the two 2X4s and place a bolt in place. You have now attached the tiller. You can also create a locking mechanism if you like to keep the tiller rigid when in use. See Figure Seventeen below about the steps for making the tiller.

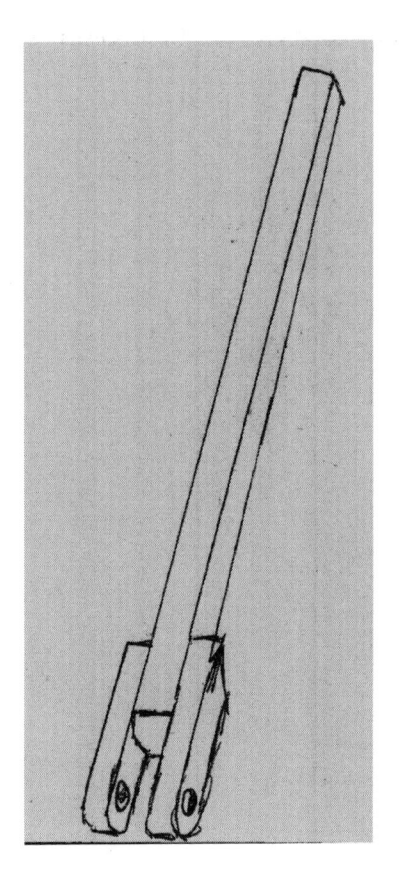

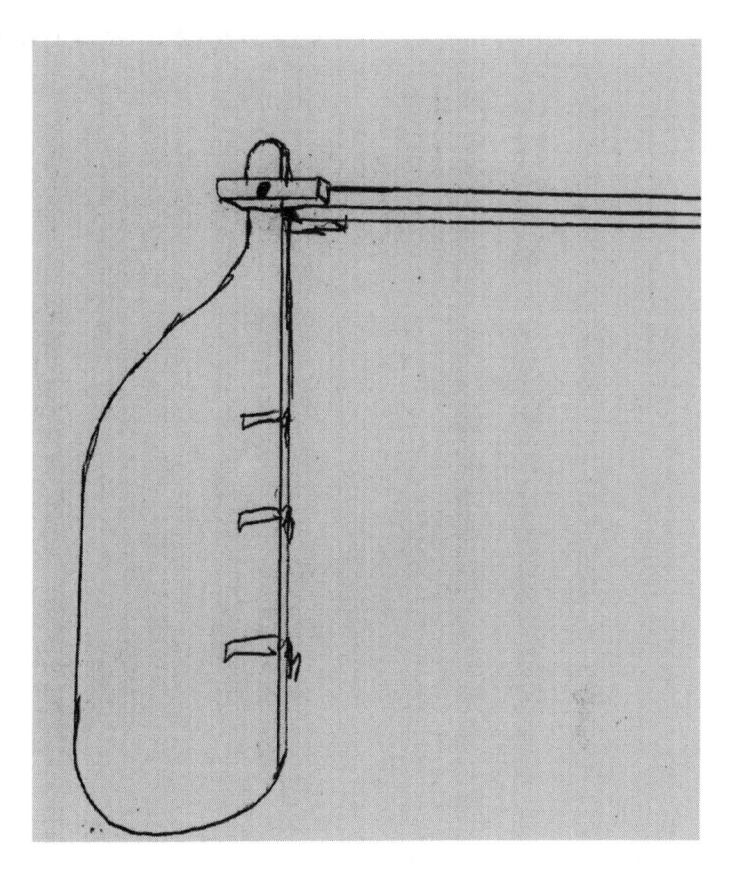

Figure Seventeen: Attaching the tiller to the rudder
Figure 17a   Figure 17b

As you notice in Figure 17a, the two 2X4s are used as a fastener for the tiller to the rudder. Then using a bolt, you can allow the tiller to pivot and lock it into place when the rudder is in use, illustrated in Figure 17b.

When building a boat, you have a unique project which is fun for the whole family. There are many resources available to build larger boats, however, this is a dying art.

Printed in Great Britain
by Amazon.co.uk, Ltd.,
Marston Gate.